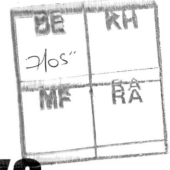
Coastal Walks
around Britain

Coastal Walks
around Britain

Andrew McCloy

Photography by Stephen Whitehorne

NEW HOLLAND

First published in 2005 by
New Holland Publishers (UK) Ltd
London • Cape Town • Sydney • Auckland

www.newhollandpublishers.com

Garfield House
86–88 Edgware Road
London W2 2EA
United Kingdom

80 McKenzie Street
Cape Town 8001
South Africa

14 Aquatic Drive
Frenchs Forest, NSW 2086
Australia

218 Lake Road
Northcote, Auckland
New Zealand

ISBN 1 84330 897 5

Publishing Manager: Jo Hemmings
Senior Editor: Kate Michell
Copy Editor: Mari Roberts
Assistant Editors: Kate Parker, Rose Hudson
Cartographer: William Smuts
Designer: Gülen Shevki-Taylor
Indexer: Dorothy Frame
Production: Joan Woodroffe

Reproduction by Pica Digital Pte Ltd, Singapore
Printed and bound in Singapore by Kyodo Printing Co.
(Singapore) Pte Ltd

Pictures appearing on the Cover and prelim pages:
Front cover: *Old Harry rocks, Dorset.*
Spine: *Seven Sisters, Sussex.*
Back cover: *Secluded cove at Porth Curno, Cornwall.*
Page 1: *Igneous rock formations at Kildonan, Isle of Arran.*
Page 2: *Dunstanburgh Castle on Northumberland's unspoilt shores.*
Right: *Rhossili Bay as seen from Worms Head, the Gower.*
Pages 6–7: *Beadnell Bay, Northumberland.*

Contents

Introduction

According to the Ordnance Survey, the coastline of mainland Britain as measured along the mean high-water mark extends to 11,072 miles (17,818km). Now, that's an awful lot of coast, and, as you would expect, it includes a huge variety of scenery and habitat. From immense, towering cliffs to unblemished sandy bays, shingle banks to saltmarsh and mudflat, promenade to fishing port, the British shoreline is a truly diverse and magnificent place to explore on foot.

A significant amount of the coast is accessible to walkers, with waymarked coastal paths ranging from the mammoth 630-mile (1,014-km) South West Coast Path around all of Devon and Cornwall (and some of Somerset and Dorset, too) to shorter, local trails such as the

Durham Coast Path and Glamorgan Heritage Coast Path. In addition to south-west England, you can continuously walk almost the entire seaboards of Fife, North Yorkshire, Norfolk, Suffolk, the isles of Wight, Man and Anglesey, Pembrokeshire, Lancashire and Cumbria.

But whether you hike for a week, ramble for a day or just saunter about for a couple of hours, the infinite variety of our shores offers something for everyone. After you've explored the routes featured here, take yourself off to the Lizard, Spurn Head, the Lleyn Peninsula, Kent's white cliffs, the Isle of Wight Coast Path and the quiet Lothian shores. And don't overlook the endless opportunities on Scotland's West Highland Coast and among its numerous islands.

The coast is an ever-changing landscape, and the walks in this book reveal how it is constantly being re-shaped – sometimes to spectacular effect. Geologists and fossil-hunters will be in for a treat, but birdwatchers' fingers will also be twitching at the prospect of sea eagles in north-west Scotland, choughs in Wales and avocets and marsh harriers in England. A walk by the sea is also a chronicle of our maritime history, from historic lighthouses and docklands through to Napoleonic Martello towers and Second World War defences, not to mention a proud fishing heritage and the ongoing popularity of the classic British seaside resorts. Despite modern development there's still plenty left untouched, thanks in no small measure to the likes of the National Trust's Neptune Coastline Campaign.

Whether you're an idle paddler or a yomping hiker, there's a bit of coast for everyone, but do remember that it's a dynamic environment and treat it with respect. If you're accompanied by dogs or small children, remember that cliff edges are often unfenced and prone to erosion, and gusting wind can make them especially hazardous in bad weather. Also stay alert to the state of the tide, and if in doubt err on the side of caution and avoid situations where you might be cut off. Tide tables are available from most tourist information centres, or go to the UK Hydrographic Office's on-line tidal prediction service at www.ukho.gov.uk/easytide.html.

Finally, two personal pleas: don't feed the seagulls, since it only encourages them to scavenge; and every time you pass a lifeboat station, drop a coin or two in their donations box – they do a first-class job and, as you'll find when you walk it, they have a lot of coast to cover.

Left: Whitby, on the North Yorkshire coast, is steeped in fishing and maritime history. It has the atmospheric remains of a 13th-century abbey and was once a leading whaling port, as well as being the base for Captain James Cook's historic 18th-century voyages to the New World.

WEST CORNWALL

T he Land's End peninsula is a singularly special place. Certainly the scenery is second to none: soaring cliffs and headlands, exquisite sandy bays and the Atlantic Ocean crashing into the rocks at your feet. Then there's the legacy of the tin-mining industry, with the derelict and rather haunting workings that cling to the cliff edge, and the profusion of flowers and migrant birds attracted by this extreme location. And, for a region annually bathed in tourists, there's also a surprising amount of peace and solitude on what, at times, can feel like a very isolated and remote coastline.

Walking to the Tip of Britain

There's something unique about the Land's End peninsula, and although I've walked around it several times I've never quite put my finger on what that extra special quality is. I think it must have something to do with being at the most south-westerly point in Britain – the end of the land in every sense. As with John o'Groats, there seems to be a clear but inexplicable pull towards the furthest piece of terra firma. On my last trip I was standing next to the First and Last House, on the Land's End clifftop, when an old American gentleman came up to me. He wanted to know, with some urgency, was this the furthest he could go? Was he the most westerly man in England? I told him he most certainly was, and once he had gone off with a satisfied smile, I gazed out at the endless ocean and it struck me that the next place you come to might well be his home. And just for a second it all made some sort of sense. But the moment passed, and I went off in search of a cup of tea. These are the sorts of illuminating experiences you have when you walk around the Land's End peninsula.

Right: This famous carving of a mermaid, reputed to be over 600 years old, can be found on a bench in Zennor Church.

Wind in Your Hair

The walk starts at Porthcurno, but if you want to tack on an extra day you could begin at Penzance and follow the coast path via Lamorna Cove. There's a decent bus network serving many of the villages along this part of the Cornwall coast, with most of the routes emanating from Penzance. One of the most regular daily services is from Penzance to Land's End via Porthcurno.

The bus stop in Porthcurno is by the car park above the beach, so that you step virtually straight onto the coast path. However, you may choose to pause and look around first, for the village has a long history as a communications centre. One of the first ocean cables from overseas came ashore here (all the way from Bombay, no less), and for a

Previous pages: Whitesand Bay, north of Land's End, offers 2 miles (3km) of golden beach and is very popular with surfers.

WEST CORNWALL

Start: *Porthcurno*

Finish: *St Ives*

Distance: *30 miles/48km*

Time: *18 hours/3 days*

Terrain: *Dramatic and frequently challenging cliff path, with some steep climbs and rough ground, particularly in the last third of the route.*

Ordnance Survey map: *Explorer 203 Land's End & Isles of Scilly.*

Guidebooks: South West Coast Path National Trail Guide: Padstow to Falmouth *by John Macadam (Aurum Press);* The South West Coast Path Guide *(information and accommodation), produced annually by the South West Coast Path Association.*

Public transport: *Public Transport Guide by Cornwall County Council (free), available locally or from Passenger Transport Unit, County Hall, Truro. Also see www.cornwall.gov.uk.*

Information: *Penzance Tourist Information Centre (01736 362207), St Ives (01736 796297); ww.swcp.org.uk.*

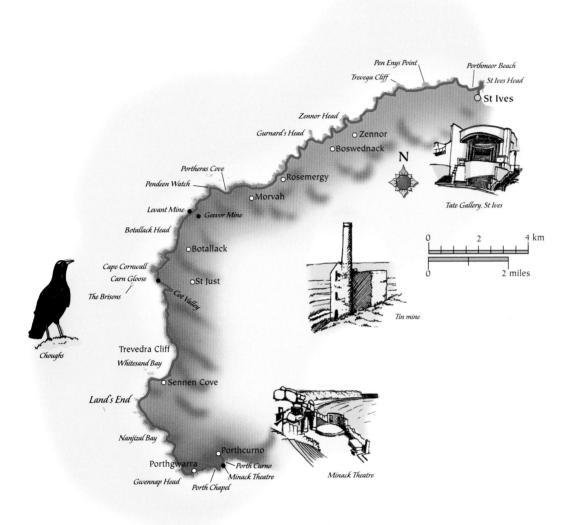

while Porthcurno Telegraph Station assumed a worldwide importance. Cable and Wireless established a training college here and 200 Cornish tin miners helped dig an underground bunker during the Second World War. All this in a tiny Cornish seaside village.

From the attractive sandy beach you are immediately faced with a climb up some very steep steps. If they look too daunting, backtrack a little and walk the easier lane onto the headland. The steps emerge by the Minack Theatre, a wonderful open-air amphitheatre fashioned out of the cliffs by Rowena Cade in the 1930s. It is open to visitors all year round and stages performances from May to September; the views over Porthcurno Bay to the Logan Rock are spectacular. Once you've regained your breath, continue westwards on the clear path along the cliffs and down to the tiny but stunning sandy cove of Porth Chapel.

After another burst of clifftop, the next descent is to Porthgwarra, a tiny fishing village where there are seasonal refreshments and toilets. The short tunnel down to the beach was dug to enable farmers to gather seaweed from the shore to spread on their fields. The coast path now leaves the sunbathers behind and takes off on a scenic and exhilarating clifftop journey to Land's End. The route is undulating but mostly obvious. Gwennap Head marks the most southerly point on your Cornish odyssey, the high clifftop topped by a coastguard station and navigational

Above: *The Minack Theatre at Porthcurno, which was created in the 1930s by Rowena Cade, stages open-air performances throughout the summer.*

aids known as daymarks that warn passing shipping of the dangers of the notorious Runnel Stone a mile offshore – they line up with the position of the reef. Beyond this the path fringes a surprisingly extensive area of heather moorland, and it feels quite remote and unpopulated. Mind you, most of the time your attention will be turned seawards, since the cliffs have been subject to folding and erosion, resulting in odd zigzag strata and spectacular natural arches. The flora and fauna can be pretty good, too, but what you see depends somewhat on the season and the prevailing weather. I have walked this path in shorts (and not much else) on a sweltering July day, standing transfixed above Nanjizal Bay as a basking shark swum to and fro in the sparkling waters below me. How different to that March afternoon when I was wrapped in a fleece and waterproofs and, bending double, attempted to make some sort of headway against a ferocious wind that even sent the seagulls hurtling backwards. Ah – the unpredictable joy of coastal walking!

At the End of the Land

By now you will be swinging irresistibly round to the north as you approach the tip of the peninsula. The complex at Land's End itself will have been visible for some time, its rather bizarre towers and shapes sitting squarely and not especially attractively on the cliff edge like a miniature Disneyland. Its blatant commercialism is not to everyone's taste, but unlike those arriving by car you don't have to pay to walk through the premises, and it is certainly a useful place to get a cup of tea and enjoy a comfort stop. If you can put up with the crowds wandering aimlessly about, visit the interesting exhibition about the Land's End to John o'Groats journey, since the club for successful 'End to Enders' is based here at Land's End.

Once you've taken it all in, and perhaps posed by the famous signpost (there's a charge to do so, of course), wander on along the cliff path towards Sennen Cove. Offshore is Longships Lighthouse, perched on a fearsome-looking reef; if conditions are clear you may be able to see the Scilly Islands 25 miles (40km) away.

All of a sudden you crest a hill and ahead is the glorious, golden sweep of Whitesand Bay, with the village of Sennen Cove immediately below. On the way down to the seafront you pass the boathouse of the Cape Cornwall Pilot Gig Club and the Round House art shop and Capstan Gallery. The Round House was formerly a net loft for local fishermen, and the Capstan below it refers to the winding gear that was used to winch the boats up the beach (a piece of equipment derived from the mining industry). The mines have all gone, of course, and only a few small fishing boats remain; the mainstay of the local economy is now tourism, as demonstrated by the range of Cornwall's artistic talent showcased at the shop and gallery. Close by is the recently renovated lifeboat station, and it, too, has an area given over to public display.

Whitesand Bay boasts over 2 miles (3km) of spotless beach. Even in the winter months there will be dog-walkers, kite-fliers or even surfers in action, for the breakers can be particularly fine on this open and exposed shore. Although the official coast path takes to the dunes at the back of the beach, the most attractive option is straight across the sand – so long as the sunbathers allow or the tide isn't racing in.

The next 3 miles (5km) of undulating cliff path are not overly difficult and include a pleasant diversion up the lush and sheltered Cot Valley near Land's End Youth Hostel. At Carn Gloose you can visit a huge chambered cairn known as Ballowall, a reminder that Cornwall is a county rich in prehistoric remains. A few miles inland is the prominent hill of Chapel Carn Brea, topped by a Bronze Age cairn; and nearby is Carn Euny, an excavated Iron Age village. This contains a 65-foot (21-metre) fogou, which is a long, stone-built underground chamber also known as a souterrain; there is another further along the coast path near Pendeen.

Exploring England's Only True Cape

Your attention will now be focused on the small, lumpy headland jutting out into the sea before you. Cape Cornwall is one of only two named capes in Britain, with the other at the opposite end of the country and visible from the Sandwood Bay walk (see pages 100–109). Technically speaking, a cape is a promontory that marks the meeting place of two channels or oceans, and this headland got its name because medieval cartographers believed that Cape Cornwall was the westernmost point in England and marked the divide between the English Channel and St George's Channel. Only later was it discovered that Land's End is in fact half a mile (0.8km) further west. The cape consists of a small but neat conical hill, topped by what at first sight appears to be a monument but turns out to be an old mining tower. If you have

Below: *The cliffs approaching Land's End are peppered with hidden, sandy coves, such as this one at Porth Curno.*

the time, it's worth walking out onto the National Trust-owned promontory for the views; one of the most entertaining outlooks turns out to be that of The Brisons, a group of semi-submerged rocks a little offshore. Their profile is such that when viewed from a certain angle they are said to look like General de Gaulle lying in the bath.

The next section, to Pendeen Watch, is a lesson in industrial archaeology, as the path passes shells of old engine houses and long-dormant chimneys. Around Botallack Head you can see some perched precariously on the actual cliff edge, a metaphor for the local industry that struggled on until 1990 when the price of Cornish tin fell so low that it was no longer economically viable to continue mining. One of the final mines to close was Geevor, which has now been opened to visitors with underground tours and an interesting guide to the surviving machinery and equipment, as well as displays of rocks and minerals from around the world. The coast path passes right through the site, and Geevor's Count House Café (open Sunday to Friday, all year round) is freely accessible and a must-stop for passing ramblers.

Geevor is a fascinating and stirring place, not least because of its location and the fact that tin mining is evidently such an integral part of the landscape and the local community. Nearby is Levant engine house, the oldest surviving mine engine in Cornwall. It has recently undergone restoration and on certain dates the beam engine is in steam. The miners' dry tunnel, which

leads to the head of what was a primitive lift mechanism called a 'man engine shaft', is also open once more, 86 years after a disaster in which 31 Cornish miners plunged to their death.

Forty Years of Protecting the Coast

A little further on from Geevor is Pendeen Watch, where a gleaming, white-painted lighthouse sits atop the prominent headland like a kittiwake on her nest. Nearby is Pendeen Manor, which does an excellent cream tea in season, while a further mile or so up the lane is the village of Pendeen, offering pubs and accommodation. Bear this in mind, because the final 14 miles (22.5km) to St Ives are breathtaking but demanding. The see-sawing cliff path involves not just plenty of ups and downs, but is also very rocky underfoot and can be boggy after wet weather. Cornwall has the longest stretch of coastline of any English county (approximately 326 miles/524km of it) and this is probably the toughest part of all. As the South West Coast Path Association guidebook says, this section will take you longer than you think.

The first bit is easy enough, with a gradual descent to Portheras Cove, a gem of a beach tucked away between the cliffs. From here the track rises and falls, and rises... Above all, though, you will see relatively few people on this long stretch. There are no cafés or caravan parks; hardly any buildings at all, in fact. It is a truly wild and unspoilt piece of coastline, exacting and rewarding at the same time.

You will not be surprised to learn that much of this unblemished chunk of coast is in the safe hands of the National Trust and, apart from a little counter-erosion work and stock fencing, human interference is kept to a minimum. The National Trust owns around 600 miles (965km) of the coastline of England and Wales, of which 413 miles (665km) have been acquired through their Enterprise Neptune Campaign. Named after the Roman god of the sea, it was launched in 1965 after research showed that a third of the coast had been developed, with 6 miles (9.5km) being lost each year. Since renamed the Neptune Coastline Campaign, the 'fighting fund' has raised a staggering £36 million, making it the most successful National Trust campaign ever, and its work to protect what is possibly our greatest natural asset continues.

Checking for Choughs

The granite and slate cliffs continue all the way to St Ives in a series of rocky headlands, covered with heather, gorse and bracken, and interspersed by deep-cut coves. The view from Gurnard's Head, in particular, captures the feel of the coastline. Because it is all relatively inaccessible and little visited, it has become a haven for wildlife, and ornithologists in particular should keep their binoculars handy. Apart from the seabirds – from fulmars and guillemots through to passing gannets – look out for peregrine falcons and the ubiquitous buzzard. You will also see plenty of jackdaws, which nest among the cliffs, and crows and rooks in the fields. But make sure to study them carefully, as one of them might be the rare chough. A medium-sized black bird, related to the crow, choughs have distinctive red feet and a curved red bill. A chough is depicted on the Cornish coat of arms (together with a fisherman and miner), but they

Below: The lighthouse at Pendeen Watch on Cornwall's north coast; all British lighthouses are now automatically operated rather than manned by a lighthouse keeper.

THE SOUTH WEST COAST PATH

The walk outlined here is only one of many fabulous coastal routes around England's south-west peninsula, all of which combine into the country's premier national trail, the 630-mile (1,014-km) South West Coast Path. This continuous route begins at Minehead in Somerset and, taking in the entire coastline of Devon and Cornwall, finally ends by Poole Harbour in Dorset.

The trail recently celebrated its 25th birthday, but in fact the cliff paths have been walked for centuries by the likes of coastguard lookouts and excise men, wreckers and writers, smugglers and shepherds. It's now one of the foremost visitor attractions in the south-west, a varied and breathtaking footpath taking in everything from urban centres, such as Plymouth and Penzance, through to fishing villages and holiday resorts. Huge headlands, such as Hartland Point, the Lizard and Prawle Point, contrast with smugglers' coves and vast, sandy bays that attract holidaymakers by the bucketload. It's a route full of highlights and with something for everyone – from Chesil Beach and Tintagel to St Michael's Mount and Newquay's surfing mecca at Fistral Bay.

It's a wonderful walk, but also a demanding one – if you complete the entire South West Coast Path you will have climbed over 91,000 feet (27,737m), which is three times the height of Mount Everest. For more information, contact the South West Coast Path Association at Windlestraw, Penquit, Ermington, Devon PL21 0LU, or go to www.swcp.org.uk.

stopped breeding in the county in 1952, since when they vanished to the remote sea cliffs of Pembrokeshire, the Isle of Man and west Scotland. In the last few years a few have returned to the Cornish cliffs, with a little assistance from local naturalists, and you may occasionally see 'Operation Chough' notices asking walkers to report sightings.

The tiny village of Zennor provides a useful staging post along this stretch, and as well as the backpackers' hostel in the former chapel (which doubles up as a café during the day) the Tinner's Arms serves a decent pint of St Austell Ale and food every lunchtime. The novelist D.H. Lawrence stayed here in 1915 and described it as 'a tiny village nestling under high, shaggy moorhills, a big sweep of lovely sea beyond, such lovely sea, lovelier than the Mediterranean'. However, Lawrence's stay was cut short when local people begun suspecting his German-born wife Frieda of being a spy, and they left rather hurriedly.

Finally the cliffs relent and St Ives comes into view, with the Tate St Ives gallery overlooking the seafront behind Porthmeor Bay. St Ives was once a busy pilchard-fishing centre, so much so that the 19th-century diarist Francis Kilvert related how the vicar of St Ives complained that the smell of fish was sometimes so strong that it stopped the church clock. The small port went on to become popular with artists and, even more so, visiting holidaymakers. After a day of tranquillity, the sheer noise and bustle of St Ives may come as something of a shock, so you may prefer to walk out to the grassy top of St Ives Head (known as the Island) and enjoy the views across the bay to Godrevy Point in peace. If you've enjoyed this taster of the South West Coast Path, how about continuing north-eastwards a little further? After all, Minehead is only 232 miles (373km) away.

NORTH DEVON

This section of the North Devon coast is stimulating but rigorous: it includes the highest spot on the entire South West Coast Path, as the huge, rounded Exmoor hills plunge into the Bristol Channel. Although the paths certainly soar, there are also some delightful pockets of woodland and numerous bays and coves, plus the traditional seaside resort of Ilfracombe. In case you don't know Devon too well, let's clear up a slight misconception. Yes, there are plenty of popular beaches thronged with holidaymakers, a good few bustling cafés serving waistline-enhancing cream teas, plus the odd caravan park here and there. But in between you will also find some of the most dramatic and impressive cliffs in England, interspersed with glorious bays that will take your breath away.

Exmoor's Wild Coast

The three walks around England's south-west peninsula featured in this book are all very different, and what will probably strike you with this Devon outing is the occasional but luxuriant tree cover, and how the wild moorland often extends down to the very cliff edge. Both these features are especially noticeable over the first day's walking.

Lynton, where the walk begins, is a small and interesting clifftop town separated from its village neighbour, Lynmouth, by the small matter of a 500-foot (150-m) drop. A unique, water-powered cliff railway joins the two, and when it was built in 1890 it was claimed to be the steepest railway in the world, with a gradient of less than one in two. Still popular today, it works using the weight of water in the 700-gallon tank of the downward car to power the simultaneous upward-moving car. Also look out for Lynton Cinema, which until five years ago was a redundant church hall and has been transformed by local volunteers into a superb 70-seat auditorium in the style of a 1930s cinema.

Right: Feral goats have roamed the Valley of Rocks, near Lynton, for many years.

Dry Valleys and Wooded Bays

The coast path leaves Lynton on North Walk, by the parish church, a route that crosses over the cliff railway and heads out via hotels and woodland for the open coast. The tarmac path was cut and laid in

Previous pages: Jagged tors line the Valley of Rocks and make the dry valley a unique place.

NORTH DEVON

Start: Lynton

Finish: Croyde

Distance: 31½ miles/50km

Time: 16 hours/2–3 days

Terrain: Undulating and sometimes steep coastal path embracing open clifftop and rocky headlands, sheltered bays and woodland.

Ordnance Survey maps: Outdoor Leisure 9 Exmoor; Explorer 139 Bideford, Ilfracombe & Barnstaple.

Guidebooks: South West Coast Path National Trail Guide: Minehead to Padstow by Roland Tarr (Aurum Press); The South West Coast Path Guide (information and accommodation), produced annually by the South West Coast Path Association.

Public transport: Exmoor Coastlink is a daily bus service linking Lynton, Combe Martin and Ilfracombe. Timetables available locally or go to www.devon.gov.uk/devonbus.

Information: Lynton Tourist Information Centre (01598 752225), Ilfracombe (0845 4583630), Woolacombe (01271 870553); www.swcp.org.uk.

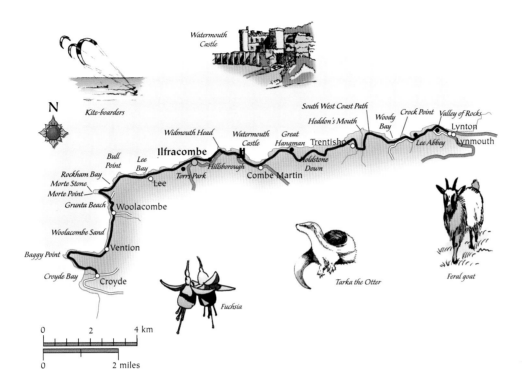

Watermouth
Castle

N

Kite-boarders

South West Coast Path
Heddon's Mouth   Woody   Crock Point Valley of Rocks
                   Bay   Lynton
Widmouth Head   Watermouth Great   Lynmouth
                 Castle   Hangman Trentishoe Lee Abbey
Bull   Holdstone
Point   Lee   Down
Ilfracombe
Rockham Bay   Lee Hillsborough Combe Martin
Morte Stone   Torrs Park
Morte Point
Grunta Beach Woolacombe

Woolacombe Sand
                                    Tarka the Otter   Feral goat
Baggy Point   Vention

Croyde Bay Croyde

Fuchsia

0   2   4 km

0   2 miles

1817, and represented the Victorians' idea of a promenade walk. Although we now tend to favour a more natural approach, the elevated views across to the Gower peninsula and South Wales are undeniably superb. Eventually, the route swings inland to enter the Valley of Rocks, a curious dry valley encircled by jagged tors and with its own herd of free-ranging feral goats. It seems more like Dartmoor than Exmoor, with the weird rock shapes bearing names like the Devil's Cheesewring and Rugged Jack. One suggestion is that the shallow valley was the original bed of the River Lyn and that, over time, coastal erosion diverted its flow out into the sea at the present site of Lynmouth.

Follow the open lane out of the valley and down past Lee Abbey, a Christian retreat and conference centre, then, after crossing the road bridge by the seasonal tearoom, veer seawards on a field-edge path round Crock Point. Beyond is Woody Bay, where well-waymarked paths and lanes guide you through predominantly oak woodland. Wandering through here on a hot summer's day, glimpsing the sparkling blue water of the unspoilt bay through the trees far below, has an almost Mediterranean feel to it.

Between Woody Bay and Heddon's Mouth is an open and exposed stretch of path, which although high on the sloping cliffs is easy to follow and not overly difficult. More great views, more wind through the hair. The track soon swings inland and drops steadily down to the River Heddon, partly disguised by a beautiful blanket of trees. At the delicate stone bridge you can divert for half a mile up the valley-bottom track to find refreshment at Hunter's Inn or the National Trust's seasonal kiosk. A short walk downstream will bring you to the pebbly beach at Heddon's Mouth, where a circular limekiln has recently been restored. In the 1800s, coal and limestone were brought across the Bristol Channel to be burnt to produce lime, which was spread on the acidic land to improve the soil. About this time, much of the woodland further up the valley was also planted, some of it destined for the return sea journey as pit props for the mines of South Wales.

Right: *Unspoilt and undulating – the North Devon coast is a delight to walk.*

Getting on Top of the Hangmen

On the far side of the river the National Trail acorn signs direct you steeply back up for the lofty walk to Combe Martin via Holdstone Down and Great Hangman. This represents the highest point of the South West Coast Path, the mammoth 630-mile (1,014-km) walking route that begins just along the coast at Minehead, in Somerset, then encompasses the entire coastline of Devon and Cornwall before finishing at Poole Harbour in Dorset.

Height rather than distance is likely to be your immediate preoccupation. At over 1,000 feet (300m), the sheer size of these two enormous sandstone hills before you – like a hog's back in shape and falling away into sheer sea cliffs – is best appreciated from further along the coast. The actual walking route is well back from the steep seaward face, and whether you charge at the slopes and lie panting at the top, or adopt a gentle pace with plenty of rests to admire the view – well, it's entirely up to you. The openness of the slopes can leave you exposed to the biting wind, however, for aside from the heather, bracken and gorse there's little tree cover, and those that do cling on have been blown into leaning, drunken postures. Despite this, a resident herd of Exmoor ponies, introduced by the National Trust to graze the rough grass and shrubs, seems quite at home here. At other times controlled burning (called 'swaling') also takes place.

The summit of Great Hangman is officially 1,043 feet (318m), and it's crowned by a huge cairn. From here a springy turf path bounds down towards Little Hangman, smaller but no less shapely. The origin of their names is uncertain, possibly a variation on the Celtic *an maen*, meaning hill of stones. A local story, probably as tall as the two hills, tells how a thief stole a neighbour's sheep and bound its legs together round his neck – then choked to death when the animal struggled. Mind you, there are certainly records of gallows having been sited on the slopes above Combe Martin. What is far more definite is that 'combe' is the Old English for valley; and from Little Hangman it's a straightforward descent to the pubs and cafés of the seaside resort for a well-earned cuppa.

Devon's Traditional Resorts

Combe Martin's small seafront is deceptive, since the village extends almost 2 miles (3km) inland along the main street, a fact that helped it enter the *Guinness Book of Records* in 2002 by hosting the world's longest street party (1½ miles/2.5km long!). Halfway up the road is a most peculiar pub called the Pack o' Cards. Built as a family home in 1690, it has four floors for the four suits, each with 13 doors for the cards in the suit, and 52 windows for the cards in a pack. Legend has it that it was built for local benefactor George Ley with the winnings from a card game.

Combe Martin represents the western end of Exmoor National Park (there's an information centre near the seafront) and it also signals a gentler stretch of coastline. The highlights of the next 5 miles (8km) from Combe Martin to Ilfracombe are Watermouth Castle (a mock Gothic construction), the views back to the Great Hangman from Widmouth Head and the exploration of the Hillsborough headland above Ilfracombe. It's as well waymarked as ever, but it is also rather bitty with some pavement walking, and if you have earmarked only two days for this walk then fast forward to Ilfracombe on the bus to resume the high-quality coast path.

Ilfracombe is a useful staging post for walkers in terms of accommodation and public transport, but the bucket-and-spade trippers will far outnumber you. The resort's popularity took off in Victorian times, and many of the elegant hotels that line the upper slopes date from this period. A curious feature to look out for are the so-called Tunnel Beaches, accessible from the town centre via pedestrian tunnels quarried through the surrounding rock by miners from South Wales. Providing safe bathing at low tide, these beaches are still used today. Ilfracombe is perhaps at its most interesting in the old harbour area, above which is the small but prominent Lantern Hill. A chapel was established here in 1320, dedicated to St Nicholas, patron saint of sailors, and the light that has been maintained here ever since is claimed to be the oldest working light in the country.

The route through Ilfracombe is intermittently sign-posted, taking a tour of Capstone Point and then out via streets beyond the Landmark Theatre and tourist

Below: The numbers of floors, doors and windows of the Pack o' Cards Inn at Combe Martin deliberately mirror the numbers of suits, card types and cards found in a pack of playing cards.

Above: Ilfracombe has been a popular destination for visitors since Victorian times.

information office (the odd-looking funnel-roofed structure). Once the houses are left behind it's a pleasant rural ramble through the National Trust's Torrs Park, an undulating strip of coastal heathland typified by clumps of gorse and bracken, and fringed by tiny coves and small jagged headlands. The underlying rock is made up of tightly packed slate, and where exposed it is frequently shattered and folded.

Wrecks and Wrecking

After an enjoyable, almost level section, a surfaced lane takes you sharply down past the old coastguard's cottage to reach the shelter of Lee Bay. Of course, shelter and concealment were also necessary prerequisites for other coastal users from the past, and the tiny coves and bays around Lee were once popular with smugglers. Ever since wool was first smuggled out of Britain when exports were banned in the 14th century, the British coast has seen a brisk trade in illegal goods. Anything from wine and spirits to tea and tobacco were fair game and, unlike the Revenue Men, these 'traders of the night' (as smugglers were sometimes known) knew all the caves and local paths.

If you're after refreshment the Grampus Inn at Lee, just five minutes' walk away, is a useful diversion. The sheltered, partly wooded combe is sometimes known as Fuchsia Valley because of the profusion of wild flowers that grow in its often subtropical climate; as you plod up the lane to rejoin the cliff path you can also appreciate some of wonderful gardens fashioned out of the hillside, one of which is periodically open to the public.

Continue past the lighthouse at Bull Point to reach Rockham Bay, with its small patch of sheltered sand. The lighthouse was built in 1879, but against the advice of the Bristol Channel pilots (who wanted it located on Morte Point itself), Trinity House decided to position it at Bull Point. Almost 100 years later part of it disappeared into the water following a major landslip, and it had to be rebuilt further up the hillside. A light vessel was brought in to provide temporary cover. As the siting of the lighthouse suggests, a number of vessels have foundered on these harsh rocks over the years, including the SS *Collier* in 1914, one of the first steamships to carry mail to Australia (although the crew were all rescued). A short way on is Morte Point, a low but dramatic headland of pale-grey rocks that tapers out into the crashing Atlantic surf. Here, too, many ships have come to grief, not least on the deadly Morte Stone with its notorious tidal race. In the winter of 1852 alone as many as five ships were wrecked on Morte Point.

Above: *Morte Point, so-called because of its treacherous rocks, viewed from Woolacombe.*

You can imagine local people huddling on the clifftop, watching helplessly as a stranded sailing ship is blown towards its deadly fate on the rocks below. Some, however, might be harbouring different ideas, as 'wrecking' was quite a popular and lucrative pastime along the North Devon coast for a rural population living a largely meagre existence. Carefully placed shore lights would lure unknowing ships not into safe harbour but onto the rocks and reefs, and as soon as the cargo was spilled it was every man for himself with little help, if any, for survivors. After a ship had gone aground so-called wreck guards were often deployed to prevent further pillage, but this spirit of wanton looting clearly continues to this day. The 114-ton cruiser *Rossekop II*, which was beached at Airy Point near Braunton in November 1972, lost most of its fixtures and fittings within a few weeks, and when the salvagers finally removed it they found that even its compressor and propeller had disappeared.

The path drops down almost to the water's edge, and if there's a fair swell you will have to watch your footing as the rocks can be slippery when wet. Whatever the conditions, Morte Point is a stunning setting, and it marks an abrupt shift southwards across the easy turf to Woolacombe. On the way to the village you pass above the diminutive Grunta Beach, which is said to derive its name from the wreck of a boat laden with live pigs. Most survived, including one that lived wild for up to a year, eating mainly seaweed. Or so the story goes.

Tarka's Trail

Woolacombe, like Croyde further on, is a popular village with all the usual amenities, but tends to get rather overrun in the height of the season. However, the star attraction is Woolacombe Sand, 3 miles (5km) of glorious, pristine sand that is a mecca for sunbathers, surfers, kite-boarders and the rest. At the rear is a large dune system, where the National Trust has been re-introducing marram grass and laying down boardwalks in an attempt to counter years of erosion. However, it's not just tourists who have been disturbing the dunes. Before the 1940s, the area played host to a golf course, then during the Second World War it was used extensively by the military in preparations for the D-Day landings. Full-scale mock assaults took place on the beach and Morte Point was used for target practice by anti-tank guns.

Although the walk along the water's edge of Woolacombe Sand towards Baggy Point is highly enjoyable, tidal conditions do not always make it possible to resume the official coast path at the far end, at Vention, so check before you set off. The official path is actually through the dunes at the back of the beach, and this waymarked route gradually rises to become a high-level walk around the edge of Baggy Point. Whereas Morte Point is generally low and rolling, made up of rough gorse and heather, Baggy Point presents a higher and more uniform headland where arable fields give way to vertical cliffs much loved by rock climbers – it's a case of eroded slate versus resistant sandstone. From both headlands, however, there are good views (weather permitting) of Lundy Island, a 3-mile-long (5-km) granite outcrop which takes its name from the Norse for puffin. These delightful seabirds can still be seen on the island, which is owned by the National Trust and was Britain's first designated marine nature reserve. There are regular summer sailings to the island from Ilfracombe and Bideford.

By now you will have also noticed that the National Trail's acorn waymark is sometimes joined by an otter's paw print, since your coastal progress from Lynton is also shared by the Tarka Trail. Centred on Barnstaple, this 181-mile (291-km) trail traces the journeys of Tarka, the otter made famous by Henry Williamson's book. And as you wander down to Croyde past the memorial to the author, with the exquisite sandy bay spread out below and far-off views of Clovelly and Hartland Point, you can't help thinking that Henry Williamson and Tarka chose a lovely spot to live.

Below: The sandy bays at Woolacombe (pictured here) and neighbouring Croyde offer superb surfing.

Opposite: The high sandstone headland of Baggy Point separates Woolacombe and Croyde.

LITERARY DEVON

Given the sheer beauty of Exmoor and the North Devon coast, it is not surprising that over the years they have inspired many writers and poets. Romantics such as Coleridge, Southey, Wordsworth and Shelley drew inspiration from the stunning landscape, with Coleridge and Wordsworth planning *The Rime of the Ancient Mariner* during a walk from Lynton to the Valley of the Rocks.

Exmoor was also the background for Richard Doddridge (R.D.) Blackmore's tragic tale *Lorna Doone*, set during the time of James II and the Monmouth Rebellion. The writer's grandfather was the vicar at Combe Martin, and a number of well-known locations appear in the book, which is based on the activities of a real-life gang of local outlaws. For instance, the character Mother Meldrum is believed to have been modelled on a real woman, Aggie Norman, who lived in a hovel in the Valley of the Rocks. Today, her 'cave' is signposted and lies just off the coast path.

A more recent and very different story – but one every bit as popular – is told by Henry Williamson. *Tarka the Otter* describes the animal's life and times 'in the land of the two rivers' (the Taw and Torridge), and has run to over 30 editions since it was first published in the 1930s. Williamson lived at the village of Georgeham, near Croyde, where he's buried in the churchyard. An unnamed man who appears in the story walking across Baggy Point is believed to be Williamson himself.

DORSET

For the walker, the Dorset coast offers extremes: from safe, sandy beaches where you can paddle to your heart's content through to plunging cliff paths where the contours are so tightly bunched that they become an orange blur on the map. The Dorset and East Devon Coast has also been designated England's first natural World Heritage Site, and it is said that in 95 miles (153km) you can walk through 185 million years of history – the Triassic, Jurassic and Cretaceous periods – in just one week. Somewhere in the equation comes wildlife, too, of course, and the Studland Heath National Nature Reserve, through which this walk passes, is an important area of dunes and heathland that supports threatened species such as the nightjar, ladybird spider and sand lizard.

The Jurassic Coast

This short but rewarding excursion along the south coast encompasses part of the superlative South West Coast Path, which links Dorset with Somerset via the entire seaboards of Devon and Cornwall. The 630-mile (1,014-km) National Trail begins (or ends, depending on which way round you look at it) at Sandbanks, by the mouth of Poole Harbour, and its first few miles are along Studland Beach. This popular location caters not just for ramblers – sunbathers, horseriders, kite-fliers, watersports enthusiasts and many others also flock to its dazzling white beaches and sunny disposition.

There's information on the natural history of the area at the National Trust's visitor centre at Knoll Beach (including the fact that Britain's three native snakes can all be found here: the adder, grass and the rare smooth snake), and since this also includes a shop and café, it makes for a good place to start the walk. However, if you do decide to add on an extra couple of miles and begin at the far, northern end of Studland Bay beside the ferry, be aware that a section of the beach is a designated naturist area. It's been so since the 1930s, and is one of the most famous in Britain; its boundary is marked by green-topped posts and signs. Should you wish to avoid this section, follow the waymarked Heather Walk Trail behind the beach.

Right: The Romanesque nave of Studland Church, near the beginning of the walk, is just one of several interesting features of this building that it is worth diverting from the route to see.

Old Harry and his Wife

Walk along the sand towards Old Harry rocks and at Middle Beach go up the lane beside the café for a woodland path that leads to Fort Henry. This impregnable, concrete structure dates from April 1944 and was built as an observation post for a rehearsal to the D-Day

Previous pages: The chalk stacks of Old Harry rocks guard the approaches to Poole Harbour.

DORSET

Start: Knoll Beach, Studland

Finish: Lulworth Cove

Distance: 23½ miles/38km

Time: 11 hours/2 days

Terrain: Grassy cliff path, promenade and sandy bays; be aware that there are some very steep sections approaching Lulworth, with plenty of ascent.

Ordnance Survey map: Outdoor Leisure 15 Purbeck & South Dorset.

Guidebook: South West Coast Path National Trail Guide: Exmouth to Poole by Roland Tarr (Aurum Press).

Public transport: Timetables available locally or go to www.purbeck.gov.uk.

Information: Swanage Tourist Information Centre (0870 4420680); Lulworth Heritage Centre (01929 400587); Studland Beach Information Centre (01929 450259); www.jurassiccoast.com.

Note: The section between Kimmeridge and Lulworth Cove is via the MOD's Lulworth firing range, which is open to the public most weekends and at other peak holiday times such as the whole of August and bank holidays. To check opening times call 01929 404819, otherwise you may be faced with a lengthy detour inland.

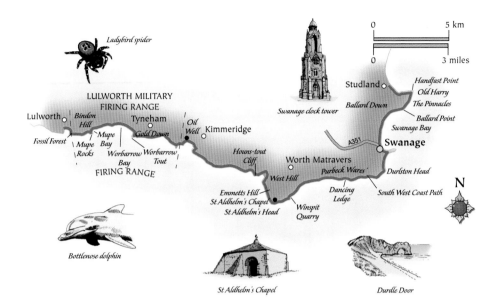

Ladybird spider

LULWORTH MILITARY FIRING RANGE

Lulworth Bindon Hill Tyneham Oil Well Kimmeridge

Fossil Forest Mupe Bay Gold Down

Mupe Rocks Worbarrow Bay Worbarrow Tout

FIRING RANGE

Houns-tout Cliff

West Hill

Emmetts Hill
St Aldhelm's Chapel
St Aldhelm's Head

Winspit Quarry

Swanage clock tower

Studland Handfast Point Old Harry The Pinnacles

Ballard Down Ballard Point Swanage Bay

A351 Swanage

Worth Matravers Purbeck Wares Durlston Head

Dancing Ledge South West Coast Path

N

Bottlenose dolphin

St Aldhelm's Chapel

Durdle Door

landings called Operation Smash. Studland was chosen because its beaches closely resemble those at Normandy, and the full-scale exercise involving warships, heavy artillery bombardments and thousands of men must have been quite a spectacle. You can still sit inside the position and gaze out of the slit windows, while nearby there is a memorial stone to the soldiers of the Royal Dragoons who died during the exercise.

Beyond Fort Henry you can either drop down to South Beach or continue on the path and then the lane past the Bankes Arms Inn. Both routes meet up on the long, straight track out to Old Harry rocks.

The best-preserved of these well-known and dramatic chalk stacks at the end of the headland is Old Harry himself, jutting proudly out of the water. Sadly, Old Harry's wife is nowadays just a stump of chalk after she was toppled by a gale in 1896. The relentless pounding of the waves on the corrosive chalk has gradually produced hollows or arches in the weaknesses of the rock, several of which can be seen here, far below the coastal path. Over time, the arches grow as the chalk is washed away, until finally the bridge collapses to form the isolated pillars of rock that are visible today.

On a clear day there are wide views back over Studland Bay towards Poole Harbour and Bournemouth, and the views are even better a little higher up at the end of Ballard Down. This lofty chalk ridge runs across South Dorset to Lulworth and – until the sea broke through a few thousand years ago – once extended eastwards to the Isle of Wight, whose high white cliffs (including the famous Needles) are often visible from this spot.

You descend gently to Swanage, the whole of the town neatly laid out around the bay below. If the tide is low you can go down the steps at Whitecliff and walk along the foreshore to reach the promenade; otherwise you must detour through the back streets for a short while before you hit the seafront.

Old London by the Sea

Swanage has become a lot more welcoming to visitors since 120 Viking longships were seen off in a foiled raid in AD 877. Since Edwardian times, the steam railway (which still runs from Corfe Castle) has brought in multitudes of trippers, but before the advent of tourism it was the stone industry that created the modern town. Highly regarded Purbeck limestone (sometimes called Purbeck marble, rather confusingly) was quarried locally and used in such prestigious national buildings as Westminster Abbey and Canterbury Cathedral. After delivering their heavy cargo, the ships from Portland needed some sort of ballast for the return leg to prevent them from capsizing, and those delivering to London found it in the discarded street furniture that the fast-expanding Victorian capital was throwing out almost daily. So it was that all manner of London's unwanted gas lights, street bollards and general masonry from long-lost statues and bridges found its way back to Swanage, soon nicknamed 'Old London by the Sea'. If you look carefully, you can still see items dotted around the town, including frontages and columns from the original Billingsgate Fish Market. The ornate stone façade of the Town Hall

Right: *The Pinnacles, between Handfast Point and Ballard Point, are testimony to the corrosive power of the waves on the chalk cliffs.*

came from the former Mercers' Hall in London's Cheapside, while the clock tower was once to be found in Southwark. For more details, pick up a town trail leaflet at Swanage Heritage Centre, near the main seafront and open every day from Easter to the end of October.

To resume the coast path follow the smart new walkway past the sailing club and diving centre and out to Peveril Point. Now the route swings south to Durlston Head, first along open clifftop through a small park, then, because a cliff fall has permanently blocked the path, via a couple of residential roads. Tranquillity is soon restored as the coast path heads off into the woods of Durlston Country Park and out to the Victorian 'castle' on the headland.

Dolphin Watching

Back on the clifftop once more, you will notice several Dolphin Watch shelters. It's all part of the Durlston Marine Project, a research and education initiative focusing on the voluntary marine nature reserve that stretches 15½ miles (25km) along the Dorset coastline to St Aldhelm's Head. Since 1998, the Dolphin Watch team has been assiduously recording sightings, and in their best year dolphins were seen as often as every three days. Most are bottlenose, but sometimes you may see a common dolphin, harbour porpoise or pilot whale. The best months to see dolphins are April, May, October and November, and the wooden shelters have

Above: *The ornate stone frontage of Swanage Town Hall originally came from the former Mercers' Hall in London's Cheapside.*

charts and pictures to aid identification. Potential dolphin-spotters are advised to have upon them binoculars to identify the shape of the fins, a pencil and notepad to record the details, warm waterproof clothing '… and lots of patience!'. As you scrutinize the deep blue waters of the English Channel, the clues to look out for are patches of white water, gulls and gannets in close attendance, and the tell-tale sign of a small, dark triangular fin. Over the last few years the project has been amassing some interesting information, including the fact that the same group of dolphins ('the Durlston Five') kept returning to the waters off Durlston Head. There's a lot more about dolphin-watching at the visitor centre, and if you have been lucky enough to see one don't forget to record it in their marine diary.

Beyond the lighthouse the path becomes more open and rugged, with Dorset County Council's country park giving way to a succession of National Trust estates. The two bodies work in partnership, managing what in fact is the largest area of coastal limestone grassland in Europe, known as the Purbeck Wares (a 'ware' being a coastal field).

Although peaceful today, it does bear the scars of past industry, since it was once a busy area for local quarrying. At its peak in the early 1800s, the clifftop quarries at Tilly Whim, Dancing Ledge and Winspit produced 50,000 tons a year of Portland stone and Purbeck limestone, which, because of a geological fault, occur here at sea level. The stone was used for a variety of purposes, with the best going into public buildings as ornamental columns and flooring, and the low-quality ending up as paving slabs. Today, the quarries are all silent, save for the jackdaws and bats and intrepid groups of climbers. One of the most accessible and revealing quarries to look around is at Winspit, which was worked up until the 1950s, and where you can see how the rock was hewn out of the sheer cliff-face, forming low caves supported by crude pillars. The rock was then lowered into the waiting boats, though if conditions were hazardous the stone was first placed in flat-bottomed craft that were then rowed out to larger vessels further offshore.

With no settlements on the coast until you reach Kimmeridge, the village of Worth Matravers (a mile inland from Winspit or Seacombe Bottom) is a useful destination for refreshments. There's a shop and café, and also a splendid old pub called the Square and Compass. Run by the same local family since 1907, it is a traditional inn that serves beer straight from the cask and has none of the modern trappings that make some of today's pubs feel uniform and characterless. It even has its own museum, including an extensive collection of rocks and fossils gathered from around Purbeck. Outside, the beer garden consists of tables and benches made from local Portland stone, as well as various mining and farming relics, such as an old wooden press. Also look out for the Egg, a giant stone sculpture made out of hundreds of pieces of loose rock by a local drystone waller.

THE JURASSIC COAST

The World Heritage Site includes not just the Purbeck area covered by this walk, but also the fossil-rich cliffs around Lyme Regis and Charmouth, the Isle of Portland and the stunning natural phenomenon of Chesil Beach. It's all worth exploring, for the varied and fascinating rock structures provide a key insight into how and why our landscape looks like it does. For instance, you'll see the dominance of the older, harder rocks like Portland limestone, which today is such a well-known building material, and around Lulworth, in particular, you can get a close-up view of the upthrust and folding of the rock strata. A walk along this so-called Jurassic Coast also demonstrates the ongoing changes that are constantly reshaping the terrain and how the sea erodes the weaker rock to form stacks and arches while at the same time building up shingle banks and depositing shells.

Some coastal locations are also rich in fossils, with one of the most unusual examples being the Fossil Forest near Lulworth Cove. Circular, hollowed lumps of rock once contained tree stumps of a forest that grew here around 140 million years ago. If you want to explore the coast for specimens remember the basic rules: don't hammer or dig in the cliffs; check the weather and tides before you set off; stay away from the foot of cliffs and use your eyes – some of the best fossils are actually found in loose material on the beach and among the pebbles and boulders.

Keeping Watch

Finally you reach the prominent headland of St Aldhelm's Head, where there is a tiny Norman chapel dedicated to the first Saxon Bishop of Sherborne. It's a simple but robust structure with a wonderful vaulted roof, although its positioning has puzzled many people. The angles of the building (rather than, as is customary, the sides) line up with the cardinal points of the compass, prompting speculation that apart from a religious purpose it may also have served some sort of defensive or even navigational role. Today, the latter job is carried out by the more modern facility next door. The lookout station on the tip of the headland is manned by the National Coastwatch Institution, a voluntary body set up in 1994 to provide HM Coastguard with a visual and radio distress watch around the home shores. The watchkeepers are fully trained and in position every day of the year, scanning the waters for any sign of trouble. The two cheerful chaps I spoke to in the St Aldhelm's Head lookout told me that their busy time is, rather predictably, during the

Above: *Beyond St Aldhelm's Head the coast path becomes progressively steeper.*

summer, when the Channel is often awash with pleasurecraft. If their door is open when you pass, make sure to say hello and drop a coin or two in their contributions box outside.

The lookout is well sited, because now the full sweep of the West Dorset coast is revealed, with the huge, swelling cliffs rising and falling for miles ahead, and culminating in the lumpy outline of Portland jutting out into the sea beyond Weymouth. It's an inspiring sight, although your excitement might be slightly tempered by the realization that you will have to walk up and down some of those daunting slopes. The first is provided by Emmetts Hill, where fortunately a long flight of steps makes the going a little easier.

Beyond the tiny, walled memorial garden to the Royal Marines on West Hill, the official coast path detours up the valley inland before returning to the clifftop via a farm track, even though there is a steeper, more direct alternative via Chapman's Pool far below. Your legs may appreciate the easier gradients of the official route, since it's another steep climb over Houns-tout Cliff before a straightforward path to Kimmeridge.

Above: *Chapman's Pool, below the slumped shale of Houns-tout Cliff.*

One of the reasons that the coast path avoids dropping right down to Chapman's Pool is because of landslips. As you will have noticed, we have moved from the chalk of Old Harry to the tough Portland limestone, and now the predominant rock changes again to Kimmeridge Clay. In fact, the slumped, dark slopes below Houns-tout Cliff are made up of unstable shales, which, because they are topped with porous limestone, become saturated and periodically slide away causing major rockfalls.

The change in rock is also evident at Kimmeridge Bay, where dark, rocky ledges extend out into the sea. This also makes accessing the marine wildlife much easier, and Dorset Wildlife Trust's information centre is a useful pointer towards such local species as the black-faced blenny, a rare fish found in these parts. You will also notice that the rocks here contain an oilfield, as evident from BP's 'nodding donkey' that has been unobtrusively pumping oil from a well on the far side of the bay since 1959.

Coves, Arches and Fossil Forests

At Kimmeridge you enter the military firing range, which as the note on page 32 explains is open most weekends (although check before you set off, since the inland detour is longer and less scenic). The 6-mile (9.5-km) coast path to Lulworth is clearly waymarked through the range by yellow-topped posts, but you must stick to the designated route because of the danger of unexploded shells – although the sheep appear to roam freely! However, there are other linking 'range walks' as well, one of which leads to the deserted village of Tyneham. In 1943, Churchill ordered that the village should be appropriated for military manoeuvres, so all the residents were evacuated as the tanks rolled in. Unfortunately, they've never rolled out and, although it is 'open' to visitors on certain days, Tyneham remains in the hands of the Ministry of Defence and the buildings (including a church) are still empty, despite years of protests by former residents.

The coast path continues its rollercoaster progress westwards, over some dramatic if sometimes steep and taxing paths. The eroded slope of Flower's Barrow, where the Iron Age hillfort has partly slid into the sea, and the sentinel whalebacks of Gold Down and Bindon Hill are among the highlights.

Towards the end of the range there are steps down the cliff to the famous Fossil Forest (see feature on page 36), beyond which the scallop-shaped Lulworth Cove appears below. To reach the far side you can either drop down to the shingle beach or climb the cliff path above, but both will give you excellent views of how the sea has forced its way in between the resistant limestone barrier and harder chalk at the back to scrape out the softer clays of the Wealden Beds in the middle. In this way the sea is creating small coves along the coast, until eventually they join together to form wider bays – as you will have seen a mile or so back at Mupe and Worbarrow Bays. A little further along the coast path is the equally famous Durdle Door, a near-perfect example of a coastal arch. If your geological appetite is still not satiated then visit the heritage centre and pick up a memento of the Jurassic Coast. You may also appreciate a rest – several million years of history in a couple of days can take a lot out of you.

Below: *The coastal arch of Durdle Door, west of Lulworth Cove.*

SUSSEX

*T*he resort of Eastbourne marks an extremely civilized beginning to one of the classic coast walks, and a stroll along its promenade is the perfect warm-up for the big hills ahead. The billowing chalk downland of Beachy Head and the Seven Sisters are not just well-known landmarks to seafarers on the English Channel, but also popular recreational spots for walkers and tourists exploring this attractive part of southern England. It's unlikely you'll have Beachy Head to yourself or will complete the Seven Sisters without meeting someone else, but this is a very sociable (as well as energetic) coast walk and full of grand views and items of interest. It's also well served by public transport, with railway stations at both ends and the Hiker Biker bus linking Seaford and Eastbourne with the Seven Sisters Country Park visitor centre at Exceat.

A Chalkland Rollercoaster

There is a small plaque on the wall next to Eastbourne Pier entitled 'Walking for Health'. Part of a national campaign to reduce the high levels of heart disease, it encourages people to enjoy the 2½ miles (4km) of promenade from Princes Park to Holywell on foot, with the message that 'brisk walking helps reduce body fat' and 'walking is ideal exercise for all body shapes and abilities'. Good news indeed, as you stride briskly along the seafront past all manner of body shapes, quite a few of whom appear unlikely to aspire to imminent briskness.

Still, as promenades go, Eastbourne's is one of the most attractive and well-kept, its three tiers including long, colourful borders, an elegant bandstand and even a periwinkle stall. On the middle level there's also a kiosk devoted to weather reports, charts and a wealth of local meteorological information. It's hard to imagine that as recently as the mid-1800s Eastbourne was a small and unassuming fishing village. It was William Cavendish, the 7th Duke of Devonshire, who set about developing it as a stylish and more cultured rival to Brighton just down the coast. He wanted it to be the 'Empress of Watering Places', and even though there's been plenty of modern building work (including a new harbourside development), the space and grandeur of the traditional old resort can still be admired along parts of the promenade.

Right: The massive lamp and lens of Beachy Head's lighthouse serves to keep all Channel traffic away from the dangerous limestone cliffs.

The Beautiful Headland

To begin the walk, go up past Helen Gardens and St Bede's Preparatory School at the far western end of Eastbourne promenade and onto the open downs, following signs for the South Downs Way. This 101-mile (163-km) National Trail runs the length of the downs to Winchester, and as a pedestrian you will be following its first stage along the cliffs to the Cuckmere Valley, while horseriders and cyclists have their own bridleway alternative inland.

It may be a steep beginning, but before long the gradient relents and the grassy slopes are pleasant and easy with great views back over Eastbourne. There's open access, with tracks

Previous pages: The Beachy Head Lighthouse sits at the foot of massive chalk cliff. It was built to replace the clifftop Belle Tout lighthouse, which is now a private house.

SUSSEX

Start: *Eastbourne*

Finish: *Seaford*

Distance: *14 miles/22.5km*

Time: *7 hours/1–2 days*

Terrain: *Springy turf and well-walked paths along undulating chalk cliffs and valley bottom.*

Ordnance Survey map: *Explorer 123 South Downs Way (Newhaven to Eastbourne).*

Guidebook: Walking the Coastline of Sussex *by David Bathurst (S.B. Publications).*

Public transport: *Sussex Heritage Coast Travel & Leisure Guide (free booklet with timetables of Eastbourne–Seaford Hiker Biker bus, etc), available locally and from Seven Sisters Country Park Visitor Centre.*

Information: *Eastbourne Tourist Information Centre (01323 411400), Seaford (01323 897426); www.vic.org.uk (South Downs Virtual Information Centre).*

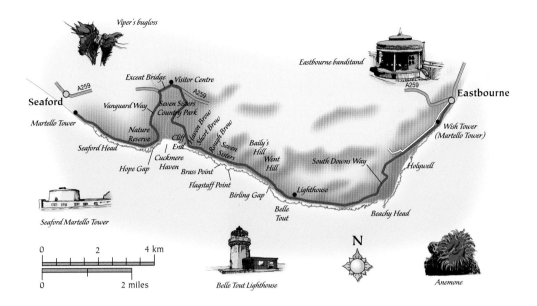

going off in several directions, but if you're in any doubt, follow signs for the South Downs Way, or simply aim for the inevitable ice-cream van at the top of the hill.

Beachy Head may not be the highest point on the Channel coast, which is at Golden Cap in Dorset, but the lofty, 500-foot (152-metre) chalk cliffs certainly have a palpable airiness to them. With good visibility the views extend as far east as Dungeness and west to the Isle of Wight, inland over the open rolling downs towards the Weald of Sussex and Kent, and even across the Channel to France on an exceptionally clear day. There will most likely also be plenty of people out enjoying picnics, flying kites or just ambling aimlessly around after an obligatory visit to the Beachy Head pub or tearoom. Some follow signs for the short circular Peace Path, dedicated to the United Nations International Year of Peace, although why this should be located on top of an isolated hill by the East Sussex coast beats me.

Beachy Head's name is believed to derive from *beau chef*, meaning beautiful headland, although sailors knew it as the Devil's Cape because of the dangerous shallows at its foot. The

Left: *Eastbourne's elegant 1000-foot (305-metre) long pier, designed by Eugenius Birch, reflects the aspirations of Victorian developers to outshine neighbouring Brighton.*

43

Above: *The three-tiered promenade at Eastbourne boasts immaculate floral beds and seemingly endless rows of benches along its 2½-mile (4-km) stretch.*

clifftop walk westwards brings you to the now redundant lighthouse of Belle Tout, built in 1834 and whose 30 or so oil lamps threw a light 23 miles (37km) out to sea. However, it was often rendered useless by sea fog, so in 1902 the Beachy Head lighthouse was erected at the foot of the massive cliff face. Still working today, but automated and demanned since 1983, the famous red and white-striped tower is best observed from a vantage spot a little to the east or west, rather than from directly above.

Since its enforced lay-off, Belle Tout has had a chequered history. The cliff-edge building was first a private residence, then fell derelict, but following reconstruction in the 1950s it became threatened by creeping erosion. After a major cliff collapse one night in November 1998 that left the lighthouse virtually teetering on the edge, it was decided to take drastic action, and in March 1999 the entire 850-ton structure was raised from its foundations and pushed by hydraulic jacks on greased rails to a new base. The lighthouse now stands 98 feet (30 metres) from the edge of the cliffs – exactly the same distance as when it was originally built. Because of the relentless decay of the cliffs, estimated in places at over 3 feet (or 1 metre) a year, it's almost inevitable that the lighthouse, which remains a private residence, will need moving again within this century.

The Ups and Downs of Sussex

If all this talk of falling cliffs and sheer drops is getting some would-be walkers nervous, then be assured that there is plenty of room on the wide, grassy clifftop to journey in complete ease and relaxation. However, a public notice at Birling Gap, erected by local residents, warns dog-owners to keep their pets on a lead, as there have been several recent tragedies where dogs chasing rabbits or gulls down the steep slopes have gone straight over the edge.

At Birling Gap, which has a pub and café, there are steps down to the shingle and sand below the dipping cliffs. It's a narrow and confined strip, but it does allow a close-up look at the cliff face, and at low tide you can appreciate the shallow ledges where earlier chalk cliffs once stood. This distinctive white rock was formed under the sea around 85 million years ago by the build-up of calcareous (chalky) bodies of microscopic marine algae. Subsequently, the chalk was thrust up to form the cliffs we see revealed today.

As the Beachy Head lighthouses testify, the cliffs are a serious danger for shipping, since fast currents drive vessels towards the rocky shelf that stretches some way out from the foot of the cliffs, and since 1563 at least 25 ships have been wrecked along this stretch of coast. Among them was *The Two Brothers*, a brig carrying thousands of lemons which was wrecked at Birling Gap in November 1790. Its crew was saved, and local people collected the unusual cargo and sold them in markets all over the south-east of England. Another victim was the *Ann Amelia*, a Swedish vessel loaded with wine, which came ashore on the rocks earlier the same year. Soldiers from Eastbourne barracks were sent to unload the ship, but were ordered straight back again when it was spotted that some were tasting the produce by catching it in their hats as it leaked from cracks in the ship's timbers.

After a short, unmade track up from the houses, the glorious springy turf takes over once more, and it's time for the Seven Sisters rollercoaster. For 2½ miles (4km) the huge undulations take you up and down Went Hill Brow, Baily's Hill, Flagstaff Point, Brass Point, Rough Brow, Short Brow and Haven Brow. However, if you keep a careful count you may detect an extra crest (called Flat Hill) just above Flagstaff Point – a missing eighth sister? It's invigorating and enjoyable walking, and try as I might, in all the times I've tackled the Seven Sisters I haven't yet been able to stop myself from running full tilt down the first slope.

Despite the popularity of the Seven Sisters, the chalk grassland remains a valuable natural habitat, containing dozens of plant species. The close grazing by sheep keeps particularly invasive species at bay, which benefits the likes of orchids, kidney vetch, cowslips and viper's bugloss. In the late spring and early summer, in particular, it's a lovely picture, and there are several quieter paths that head inland across the downs and are particularly rich in wildflowers and butterflies.

Cuckmere's Delicate Future

Finally, the chalk cliffs relent and Cuckmere Haven is revealed. King Alfred the Great is supposed to have founded a shipyard here, but by the 1800s it was mainly used by violent smuggling gangs moving contraband French brandy upriver to Alfriston. At one point, gangs of smugglers 200- to 300-strong carried away illicit goods from in front of the helplessly outnumbered excise men. However, not every attempt was successful. In 1923, a plan was

Below: As you stand on the slopes of Beachy Head and look eastwards there is a wide open view towards Eastbourne and Pevensey Bay.

Above: From the mouth of the Cuckmere River, where the South Downs meet the sea, the walker has a fantastic view of the distinctive white chalk cliffs of Sussex's Seven Sisters.

Opposite: There has been a lighthouse at Beachy Head, which, at 530 feet (162m) is the highest chalk sea cliff in Britain, since at least 1670.

hatched to smuggle 91 cases of brandy from Dieppe on board a fishing boat, but thanks to bad weather the pilot suffered severe seasickness and after a torturous night at sea the boat landed at Newhaven instead of Cuckmere Haven – to be greeted by the customs men.

In 1846, the Cuckmere River was canalized to keep the river clear of silting and the valley free from flooding, but recent proposals by the National Trust have suggested returning the river to its original meandering course. It's partly a response to the frequent damage caused to Cuckmere Haven by storms, which, together with the effects of longshore drift (the natural movement of shingle eastwards along the beach by wave action), means that the sea defences have to be continually repaired and the river mouth dredged to keep it clear. The long-term vision is to allow nature to take its course by letting the river flood the surrounding fields, so gradually turning grazing pasture into saltmarsh and mudflats. It will provide a natural barrier against the threat by the sea and have benefits for wildlife such as wading birds, but if the original course of the river is ultimately to be restored it will vastly alter the whole landscape and is a weighty move. Today Cuckmere Haven remains the only river mouth between Ipswich and Southampton not to be overshadowed by retirement bungalows or caravans, nor tainted by industrial development or roads.

Enjoying the Country Park

You can see the layout of Cuckmere Haven from the top of Haven Brow, the last 'sister', and how the artificial channel runs dead straight across the lower valley. From here you have several choices, but all involve walking upstream through the Seven Sisters Country Park to Exceat Bridge, since the River Cuckmere is usually too deep and dangerous to wade. You can either drop straight down Cliff End to the pebbly beach and riverbank, or choose a low path around the hillside. Better still, enjoy the views on the higher path taken by the South Downs Way. Unless you stick to the embankment of the cut (which comes out by the bridge), the paths eventually emerge opposite the country park visitor centre at Exceat, where there is an interesting exhibition about the 700-acre (280-hectare) site that was purchased by East Sussex County Council in 1971. You will learn, among other things, that the country park is a designated Site of Special Scientific Interest and an Environmentally Sensitive Area, part of the Sussex Downs Area of Outstanding Natural Beauty, includes a Voluntary Marine Conservation Area and is a core part of the Sussex Heritage Coast, and looks likely to be included in the proposed South Downs National Park. Phew! Another important piece of information, if you've walked all the way from Eastbourne, is that located next door is a handy tearoom.

You have to walk along the pavement of the busy A259 in order to cross Exceat Bridge by the Golden Galleon pub, then make your way back out to Cuckmere Haven. One route is

along the riverbank, while a higher option follows the route of the Vanguard Way. This 66-mile (106-km) long-distance footpath runs from East Croydon to Seaford and Newhaven via the Weald, and is named after the mainly London-based Vanguards Rambling Club who pioneered the route. Their name derives from the time when, travelling back on a train from a walk in Devon in 1965, there were so many of them that they could not fit into one compartment – so they all squeezed into the guard's van instead!

Scattered about the lower valley are various pillboxes and gun emplacements that date from the Second World War. When enemy air raids began to intensify, a network of lights was erected across the valley floor in an attempt to fool German bombers into mistaking the River Cuckmere for the River Ouse and so protect the busy port of Newhaven.

In Sight of Seaford

The remainder of the walk is as straightforward as the rest: follow the wide and well-walked grassy strip along the clifftop beyond the cottages (not the unmade track inland) all the way across Seaford Head, keeping seawards of the clifftop golf course. When the tide is out an alternative from Cuckmere Haven to Hope Gap is to walk along the wide, wave-cut platform, and at low tide you can explore the array of wildlife that inhabits this fascinating environment. Look out for anemones and sponges clinging to the side of the vertical cracks, and snails and limpets grazing on the many-coloured seaweed. Molluscs, such as the shipworm and the splendidly named common piddock, bore small holes or cavities into the rock using their

---

WALKING: THE HEALTHY OPTION

The healthy walking message proclaimed on the promenade at Eastbourne may seem out of place among the ice creams and burgers, but you will almost certainly pass plenty of people out stretching their legs on the user-friendly Sussex downland that overlooks the resort. By no means everyone will be attired in boots and rucksacks and intending to walk 14 miles (22.5km), of course, but the fact that they are out and exercising is welcome news, for more and more research is showing that regular walking is good for you. Not only does it counter the risk of coronary heart disease, but it also makes for suppler joints and stronger bones. Regular walking reduces body fat and lowers cholesterol levels, and is a social and enjoyable form of exercise that promotes a state of mental well-being. Indeed, according to proponents of the 'biophilia effect' theory, walking in unspoilt green spaces reconnects us with our natural environment and relieves tension caused by the stresses of our artificial urban surroundings and hectic modern lifestyle.

Over the last few years, the Walking for Health initiative, promoted by the Countryside Agency and British Heart Foundation, has encouraged health practices across the country to introduce programmes of gentle, self-led and organized 'health walks', rather than the usual prescription of pills and medication, with an emphasis on people taking responsibility for their own and their community's health. As you amble happily across the downs of Sussex, you may care to reflect that in this age of junk food and rising levels of obesity, the basic art of walking is one obvious and simple solution.

suckers or spines (or, in the case of the sea urchin, its teeth) to help them cling on against wave action and predators.

Low-level walkers must use the steps at Hope Gap to rejoin the cliff path for the route across Seaford Head, crowned by the faint, triangular-shaped outline of an Iron Age hillfort. It's part of the Seaford Head Local Nature Reserve, which apart from an array of chalk-loving plants, such as quaking grass, scabious and bird's foot trefoil, also attracts plenty of insects like bees and moths, plus an inordinate number of rabbits whose burrows litter the fenced-off clifftop. Skylarks serenade you overhead, and look out for hovering kestrels and, in the summer, the likes of linnets and stonechats in the adjoining scrub.

All of a sudden the houses of Seaford appear below, stretching out across the bay to Newhaven, with Brighton beyond. At one time, the River Ouse emerged at Seaford and such was its importance that the port was even granted membership of the Cinque Ports Confederation. But by the end of the 1500s a build-up of shingle had made the river virtually unnavigable, until finally the mouth was pushed so far westwards that a 'new haven' was established and Seaford became effectively river-less.

The main part of the town is away from the shingle beach, and the highlight of the otherwise unremarkable seafront is a moated Martello Tower, topped by a cannon. This curious fortification is the most westerly of over 200 similar defences constructed along the coast of south-east England to counter the threat of a Napoleonic invasion (also see the Suffolk walk, pages 50–59), and after renovation in the 1970s it now contains the Seaford Museum of Local History, open over summer weekends. You may have seen a similar building on Eastbourne promenade, renamed the Wish Tower and today containing a puppet theatre. These towers put me in mind of concrete sandcastles, defying the waves like they were supposed to repulse the French; and unlike the chalk cliffs of Sussex possibly standing for a little longer.

Above: The lower Cuckmere Valley, through which the River Cuckmere meanders spectacularly, forms part of the Seven Sisters Country Park, and is an important area for both conservation and recreation.

SUFFOLK

Suffolk's understated coast has a quiet charm all of its own. The elegant towns of Southwold and Aldeburgh appear to actively resist the excesses of the modern seaside resort, while an out-of-season walk through villages such as Orford and Walberswick feels like a journey back into the past. The landscape, too, can be tremendously evocative, especially when the mist is swirling over the marshes and feeling its way up the rivers and estuaries that bite into this low-lying county. From shingle and reedbed to heath and woodland, the Suffolk coast is surprisingly varied, and since much is protected by a string of nationally important nature reserves, it makes for a great wildlife walk.

Resisting the Tide

Your route along Suffolk's rather vulnerable shore follows the course of the Suffolk Coast and Heaths Path, an easy 50-mile (80-km) route that links England's most easterly point at Lowestoft with the port of Felixstowe. The actual trail is more coastal than coast: it has a tendency to wander off inland through the unspoilt hinterland when a more obvious route is along the high shingle banks and narrow strips of sand. Mind you, some of the latter is only revealed towards high tide and, together with the fact that shingle can be quite a difficult walking surface, the choice of routes may be welcome. Where relevant, both are described here.

Beer from the Coast

The walk begins at Southwold, which sits on a low hill above the mouth of the River Blyth. Most of the town's charming architecture dates from after 1659, when a disastrous fire destroyed much of the original settlement. Near the neat, white-painted lighthouse, which sits back from the seafront amid the actual houses, is the Battle of Sole Bay Inn. The name relates to a largely forgotten naval battle fought in 1672 between the combined English and French fleets and the Dutch. The erosion of the headlands of Easton Ness and Dunwich means that Sole Bay itself has largely vanished and is no longer marked on maps. This, together with the fact that few records exist of a fierce maritime encounter that supposedly engaged almost 200 ships, makes the event all the more mysterious.

The Sole Bay Inn is run by Adnams Brewery, the independent Southwold brewers who incorporated the original Sole Bay Brewery many years ago. Their slogan is 'beer from the coast', which surely makes it worthy of mention in this

Right: Beer has been brewed in Southwold for more than 650 years, firstly in the ancient Swan Inn, and later in the Sole Bay brewery. The Adnams brothers bought the brewery in 1872 and their name has stayed with the beer ever since.

Previous pages: Martello Towers, such as this one at Slaughden, were built with the intention of repulsing Napoleon's invading French forces in the late 18th century. Their design was inspired by a similar defensive structure the British came up against in Corsica.

SUFFOLK

Start: Southwold

Finish: Orford

Distance: 30 miles/48km

Time: 12 hours/2 days

Terrain: Low, flat shoreline of shingle bank, dunes, heathland tracks and grassy embankment.

Ordnance Survey maps: Explorer 231 Southwold & Bungay, 212 Woodbridge & Saxmundham.

Guidebook: The Suffolk Coast & Heaths Path (pack of laminated route cards featuring maps and route description by the Suffolk Coast and Heaths Project).

Public transport: www.suffolkcc.gov.uk/transport.

Information: Southwold Tourist Information Centre (01502 724729), Aldeburgh (01728 453637); www.suffolkcoastandheaths.org.uk.

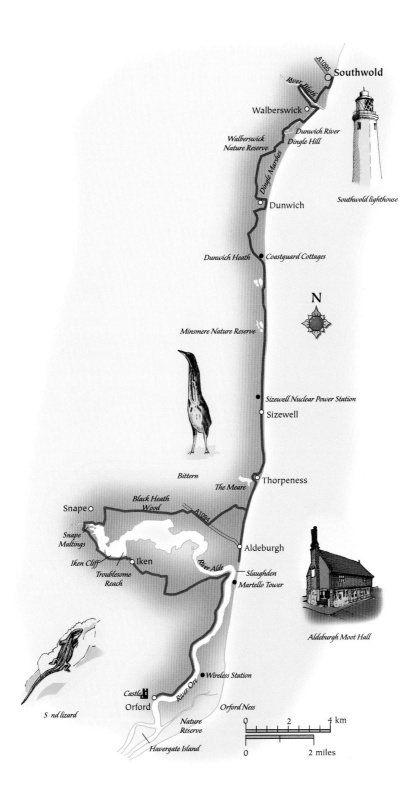

Southwold

River Blyth

A1095

Walberswick

Walberswick
Nature Reserve

Dunwich River
Dingle Hill

Southwold lighthouse

Dingle Marshes

Dunwich

Dunwich Heath • Coastguard Cottages

N

Minsmere Nature Reserve

Sizewell Nuclear Power Station

Sizewell

Bittern

Thorpeness

The Meare

Black Heath
Wood

A1094

Snape

Snape
Maltings

Iken Cliff   Iken

Aldeburgh

River Alde

Troublesome
Reach

Slaughden
Martello Tower

Aldeburgh Moot Hall

Sand lizard

Wireless Station

Castle
Orford

River Ore

Orford Ness

Nature
Reserve

Havergate Island

0   2   4 km

0   2 miles

book, and they still deliver it to the local pubs using traditional horse-drawn drays. Indeed, there's so much to distract you in Southwold – including the Sailors' Reading Room and prize-winning pier which, when it was opened in 2001, was the first to be constructed in Britain for 45 years – that it's best to leave yourself plenty of time for exploration.

Across the Marshes

Head south to the River Blyth, either along the shore or via the ferry path across the marshes, and nip across on the foot ferry or walk upstream the short distance past the boatyards and Harbour Inn to cross via the footbridge.

The route goes seawards of the quiet village of Walberswick, which once boasted a significant herring fleet, and is then waymarked out across the marshes via boardwalks. This is Walberswick National Nature Reserve, a protected area of reedbed that is among the largest of its kind in Britain. Along the way you pass the red-brick tower of an abandoned windmill, formerly used to pump water out of the marshes and into the Dunwich River. However, during the Second World War the marshes were deliberately flooded in order to prevent German gliders from landing, and now they provide a valuable habitat for birds such as sedge warblers, shelduck and marsh harriers.

A little beyond the old windmill you have a choice of routes. You can continue across the marshes on a public footpath to return to the sea bank and from here follow the

Below: Southwold's distinctive lighthouse, which stands in the centre of this historic town, was built in 1892 and is still in operation. It is open to the public from April to October each year.

shingle all the way to Dunwich. If you do so, make sure to keep out of any fenced-off areas, which from mid-April to mid-August protect ground-nesting birds such as little terns, ringed plover and avocets (their 'nests' can be virtually invisible to the human eye as the eggs deliberately resemble the stones and pebbles they sit among).

The other option is to follow the official trail via Dingle Hill and a lovely, tree-lined bridleway landwards of Dingle Marshes, a vast area of grazing marsh and brackish lagoons partly managed by the Suffolk Wildlife Trust.

Lost to the Sea

Both routes meet up again at the small village of Dunwich. Small today maybe, but once this unassuming place was the foremost port of East Anglia. As far back as Roman times, Dumnocaister had a busy harbour, and the Vikings later used it as the administrative capital of Danelaw. By the 11th century, Dunwich was the tenth largest settlement in England, but a series of violent

storms and relentless erosion by the sea caused the port's harbour gradually to silt up and the unstable, sandy cliffs to disintegrate into the waves. The town, which once boasted six churches, three chapels, two monasteries and even its own mint, fell into the sea and was abandoned, and all that remains from the original community are the battered walls of Greyfriars Friary. They say you can still hear the long-lost church bells tolling when a storm approaches, and although that may be a trifle fanciful, there have been instances of people finding human bones among fresh falls of cliff. You can learn more about the fascinating story of Dunwich in the private museum on St James Street (open daily, April–September), which includes among other things a scale model of the long-lost town as it would have looked at its medieval peak.

Present-day Dunwich does at least have a café and a pub. Once refreshed, follow the waymarked coast path across the low, wooded cliffs past the remains of the friary and out across Dunwich Heath. You may lose sight of the sea for a while, but instead you are treated to an increasingly rare coastal habitat, one of the most threatened in the country. It's a remnant of the Sandlings Heath, which once spread across East Anglia and is thought to have formed in Neolithic times after early farmers cleared the tree-cover. The sandy, acid soil proved unsuitable for crops and so the land was grazed by animals, preventing the trees from re-colonizing. The result is the heath of bracken, heather and gorse, with stands of pine and silver birch, supporting rare wildlife like the nightjar, Dartford warbler and sand lizard. The heathland interlude concludes with a return to the 'clifftop' (in so far as Suffolk has cliffs) at the National Trust's Coastguard Cottages, where there is a visitor centre and, of course, a trusty tearoom.

Above: *The River Blyth forms Southwold's southern boundary and is crossed by the seasonal foot ferry, which runs daily in the summer months and connects Southwold to Walberswick.*

THE DISAPPEARING COAST

The vulnerability of England's low-lying east coast is well documented, but the remedies for safeguarding it are not so easy to come by. The devastating floods of 1953 killed 307 people and engulfed large parts of the Lincolnshire, Norfolk, Suffolk and Essex seaboards, but coastal erosion has been eating away here for far longer. As you will see, entire communities like Dunwich have succumbed to the North Sea, while others such as Orford have been rendered economically useless by the build-up of silt and shingle banks. Elsewhere on the east coast a variety of measures have been deployed to counter the effects of the sea on the land, from building huge concrete sea walls to bulldozing new, higher beaches, even creating artificial reefs offshore in an attempt to thwart the power of the waves. But, if, as we're led to believe, global warming is now a reality, causing sea levels to rise as south-east England gradually sinks, isn't all this effort in coastal protection ultimately a waste of time? After the floods of 1953 Winston Churchill spoke of 'no surrender' to the sea, but in recent years there has been serious debate about the merits of allowing low-value coastal farmland to be flooded by the sea in order to create a natural buffer of saltmarsh (a so-called 'managed retreat'). Already this has been trialled in Lincolnshire, to the immediate benefit of wildlife, but it remains to be seen whether the human inhabitants of England's threatened east coast are equally welcoming or the local authorities quite so bold.

The Boom of the Bittern

The uncomplicated route now heads directly southwards along the coastal strip – either the sand and shingle at low tide, the high bank behind or the corridor of dunes landwards of this. The last option is probably the best, since it allows the best views of the RSPB's flagship Minsmere Nature Reserve. There's a public viewpoint halfway along the footpath, but to enter the reserve itself and benefit from the other hides and trails you must obtain a ticket from the visitor centre. It's well worth putting aside a few hours for the visit, since Minsmere boasts a carefully managed range of habitats that are rich in all manner of wildlife. Insects such as butterflies and damselflies and even mammals such as otters and water voles find refuge in the 1,560-acre (632-hectare) site, but it's the birdlife that makes Minsmere famous, typified by a pioneering, man-made lagoon system known as the Scrape that, depending on the season, may be home to avocets, redshank and godwits. In winter, the grazing marshes support huge flocks of wildfowl, plus breeding lapwing and snipes, and the majestic marsh harriers. Meanwhile, the extensive beds of reeds are one of the few strongholds left in Britain of the bittern. This shy and elusive bird is rarely seen (by other bitterns, let alone humans) but more usually heard between March and June when the male emits a deep and extraordinary booming sound to lure females.

Once you've had your ornithological fill, continue along the beach or bank top path past Sizewell Nuclear Power Station. There are actually two (Sizewell A and Sizewell B), the older gas-cooled Magnox reactor dating from the 1960s and the other a pressurized water reactor that came into service in the mid-1990s (that's the one in the giant golfballlike dome). The reactors are cooled by seawater, which is then pumped back out into the North Sea a few degrees warmer. This has given rise to what in effect are small areas of sub-tropical marine life. Sitting outside the beach café in the shadow of the gigantic, futuristic shapes, you do find yourself peering into your cup of tea with some wariness.

Carry on along to Thorpeness, a purpose-built holiday village constructed in the early 1900s. The centrepiece is The Meare, a large boating lake that was dug by hand, and which is overlooked by an 85-foot (26-metre) water tower, made all the more extraordinary as it is now a private residence known as the House in the Clouds.

Aldeburgh's Genteel Charm

Just under a mile south of Thorpeness, the Suffolk Coast and Heaths Path leaves the shoreline and heads cross-country to begin the long detour round the Alde estuary. However, it would be folly indeed to miss out on the charms of Aldeburgh, so continue along to the elegant buildings and beach-side fishing huts of this, the most genteel of resorts. Look out for the 16th-century Moot Hall, which stands rather incongruously on its own near the model yacht pond, and the slender lookout tower on the edge of the beach, which today houses an art gallery. The celebrated physician Elizabeth Garrett made history in Aldeburgh by becoming Britain's first woman mayor in 1908, while the port's highly regarded shipbuilders (based to the south at Slaughden) were responsible for Sir Francis Drake's *Pelican* and *Greyhound*. Not every idea worked, however. In 1870 a local man came up with the idea of drilling holes in the side of his ship so the hold would fill up with water and the newly caught cod would stay alive until he returned to port – it didn't catch on.

The diversion round the estuary of the River Alde includes a long, peaceful stretch through Black Heath Wood, preceded by a marshy area that hums with dragonflies in summer. The route is known as the Sailors' Path, and was once used by fishermen walking to Aldeburgh to go fishing for herring and sprat. Approaching Snape, the waymarked trail heads out across Snape Warren and a lovely oak-covered hilltop, then out on a path among the reedbeds to Snape Maltings. In 1840, Newson Garrett (father of ten children, including suffragette Millicent Garrett Fawcett and aforementioned Elizabeth) set up a malting business at this location, but today the venue is better known for its music, since Benjamin Britten's Aldeburgh Festival of Music and the Arts moved here in the 1960s. The centrepiece is the 830-seat concert hall, located on the site of the original grain-drying hall where the malt was dried in kilns. The annual Aldeburgh Festival continues to thrive, although there are performances at Snape Maltings all year round, and the sizeable centre is also home to an array of craft shops and galleries.

Below: The RSPB's Minsmere Reserve is home to an array of wildlife, but is especially well known for its avocets, marsh harriers and the rare booming bittern. There are nature trails through the various habitats.

Above: Aldeburgh's shingle shoreline stretches flat and straight towards Thorpeness and Sizewell.

Now the route crosses fields beyond Snape Maltings to reach a particularly fine estuary-side section at Iken Cliff. In between the peaceful marshes there are extensive mudflats, much loved by wading birds, although not by local barge sailors who once carried loads of corn bound for the London markets. Stretches of the River Alde off Iken Church are still known as Long Reach and Troublesome Reach, and wooden stakes known as withies were embedded in the mud in an effort to guide ships along the proper river channel. Over time, the banks of the river were built up to enable surrounding marshland to be drained and prepared for farming, but in the great floods of 1953 (see the feature on page 56) high tides breached the bank between Iken and Snape and created the mudflats you see today. You can still see some of the old gateposts and dead trees below the high-tide mark, reminders of the former fields that were inundated.

After a section along a series of deserted lanes, the route returns to the water's edge via Lamberts Lane and a bridleway out to the open, grassy bank of the River Alde almost opposite Aldeburgh, the town you left some time ago. From here to the end of the walk at Orford you follow the raised embankment as the river is forced southwards from its original exit point near Aldeburgh by the longest shingle spit in Europe. Stretching almost 10 miles (16km), the spit runs from Slaughden to North Weir Point, and is formed by the ongoing movement of shingle by the sea at the rate of around 16 yards (14.6 metres) every year.

As you will have noticed by now, shingle plays a significant part in the make-up of the Suffolk coast (there's even a place south of Orford called Shingle Street), but for all its visual dullness it provides a unique natural habitat, especially above the high-water mark where it is less prone to the actions of the sea. So-called vegetated shingle is found in very few places in the world, and Suffolk accounts for over 20 per cent of Britain's share. Typical shingle plants include sea campion and biting stonecrop, plus other hardy plants such as yellow-horned poppy and sea kale. The latter, which is a member of the cabbage family, has large, waxy grey-green leaves and was once eaten as a vegetable. So, too, was the sea pea, which looks a lot like its allotment equivalent, and in 1555 was said to have kept the inhabitants of Orford alive after crop failure and famine drove them to eating the wild plants of the seashore.

Orford Ness and its Curious Buildings

As you wander southwards along the easy but invariably empty embankment, enjoying the open spaces with light reflecting off the water and the sound of skylarks trilling in the air above, you'll notice a succession of fascinating man-made structures on the diminishing spit opposite. The first is the Martello Tower at Slaughden. Over 200 of these remarkable defences were built around the coast of (mainly) Suffolk, Essex, Kent and Sussex in the late 19th century, as fears of a French invasion mounted. The round, thick-set stone towers, containing guns and magazines, derive their name from an original fortification built, rather ironically, by the French at Mortella Point on the island of Corsica, and which impressed the British command after repulsing a two-day attack by their warships.

Below: Boats are frequently moored in the River Alde by Snape Maltings, a former malt-house that has been converted into a concert hall and arts centre.

The second distinctive, and strikingly ugly it has to be said, building you will see opposite used to be a radio research station, and the forest of tall masts near it is still used to transmit BBC World Service programmes. Next is the lighthouse, and beyond this are two curious pagoda-like structures that were built by the military for the testing of atomic detonators (the thinking being that if something went badly wrong the pillars would be blown out and the heavy roof would crash down and seal everything). When the Ministry of Defence ceased using the site in the late 1980s they sold it to the National Trust, and today you can walk on to part of Orford Ness from Slaughden, or take a boat trip from Orford quay around Havergate Island, owned by the RSPB and famous for breeding avocets and little terns.

The best way to appreciate the sheer size and peculiar layout of Orford Ness is to climb the 91 steps of Orford Castle's impressive keep (all that remains of Henry II's original fortress). You will see the course of the coast path as it continues south via Shingle Street and the ferry over the mouth of the River Deben at Bawdsey to finish at Felixstowe, about 14 miles (22.5km) distant. But for now relax and explore the handsome village of Orford, with its tidy red-brick cottages, museum and two old pubs; or possibly call by the Oysterage, where you can sample the famous oysters from the beds at nearby Butley. It's perhaps a rather indulgent way to end your journey along Suffolk's varied and engrossing coastline, but you may feel that after a 30-mile (48-km) walk you have earned it.

NORTH NORFOLK

*O*ne of the most appealing aspects of British coastal walking is its
infinite variety, and nowhere is this truer than along the wild
and atmospheric Norfolk shores. In contrast to the towering cliffs
and bays of the west coast, here we have vast tracts of tidal saltmarshes and
mudflats, riddled with creeks and inlets, which stretch out endlessly to the
distant horizon. There are also glorious sandy beaches and low, crumbling cliffs,
which together with constantly shifting shingle banks make up one of the
largest and richest expanses of unharnessed coastline anywhere in Britain.

From Seals to Saltmarsh

The largely undeveloped North Norfolk coast, with its string of nature reserves, is inevitably rich in natural history, especially birdlife, but it's not just the close-up detail that's absorbing. The huge skies will simply bowl you over, and the sheer space and openness of the landscape make you feel like an incredibly small dot on a very large map. Watching the play of the clouds and the effect of light and colours on the seascape can be spellbinding, especially when combined with a glorious sunrise or sunset. Atmosphere is something that this coast has in abundance.

Following the Trail

As far as practicalities are concerned, this is a pleasingly uncomplicated walk that is perfect for a linear outing. The route is well waymarked by acorn symbols and finger posts, since it forms part of the Norfolk Coast Path National Trail, which, together with the linking Peddars Way, stretches a total of 93 miles (150km) through the peaceful East Anglian countryside. For much of this 29½-mile (47.5-km) section you follow clear tracks along the edge of the marsh or on top of sea banks, while the route along the beach and shingle bank is equally obvious. In addition, the excellent Coast Hopper bus provides a frequent, daily service to all the villages and towns along the length of the walk, making for an easy and complete round trip. All you have to do is remember your binoculars.

Right: This former granary tower can be found at the harbour at Wells-next-the-Sea, which is one of the last active ports on this stretch of coast.

Previous pages: The saltmarsh habitat as found on the Norfolk coast, such as here at Burnham, is among the most important of its kind in Europe.

NORTH NORFOLK

Start: *Burnham Deepdale*

Finish: *Sheringham*

Distance: *29½ miles/47.5km*

Time: *12 hours/2 days*

Terrain: *Easy, flat edge of saltmarsh and top of sea banks; low grassy clifftop; shingle and sand dunes.*

Ordnance Survey maps: *Explorer 250 Norfolk Coast West, 251 Norfolk Coast Central, 252 Norfolk Coast East.*

Guidebook: *Peddars Way & Norfolk Coast Path National Trail Guide by Bruce Robinson (Aurum Press); accommodation guide by Norfolk area Ramblers' Association.*

Public transport: *Coast Hopper bus service provides excellent daily coverage of the whole route. Timetables available locally or go to www.passengertransport.norfolk.gov.uk.*

Information: *Wells Tourist Information Centre (01328 710885), Cromer (01263 512497), Sheringham (01263 824329), Deepdale (01485 210256); www.deepdalefarm.co.uk; www.nationaltrail.co.uk/peddarsway.*

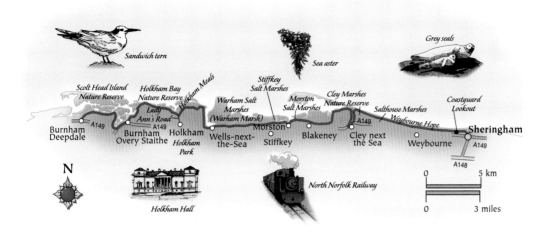

The walk begins at a useful local centre called Deepdale Information, incorporating a shop (books and maps, tourist information), café, backpackers' hostel and campsite. It's situated in Burnham Deepdale almost opposite the church on the main road, and just along from here is a short connection to the coast path. As far as further walk directions go: turn right and keep the sea on your left all the way to Sheringham!

Golden Sands and Shifting Dunes

As soon as you stride out on the broad, elevated sea wall the sense of light and space is overwhelming. The flatness of the marshes and mudflats allows your eyes to wander far into the distance, and slowly you become aware of the vastness of the sky. Underfoot the grassy bank is firm and easy to follow, so you can gaze seawards towards Scolt Head Island, a protected nature reserve of continually shifting sand dune, beach and saltmarsh. In late spring and early summer the shingle and dunes are home to thousands of terns, including the common, little and small varieties, plus up to 25 per cent of Britain's nesting sandwich terns.

The route arcs round to enter the village of Burnham Overy Staithe past a converted windmill, then heads down to the attractive quay. Further on along the main street is a pub called the Hero, its sign depicting Admiral Lord Nelson, who was born in nearby Burnham Thorpe.

Resume the meandering sea-wall path, until finally, beyond the bumpy line of dunes, you burst out onto the glorious golden beach at Holkham Bay. The coast path now turns right (east) to follow the wide, sandy strip towards Wells. Depending on the time of year, the dunes may be scorching hot and the prospect of a paddle in the cool, blue waters irresistible, or else a brisk northerly wind will be blowing in across the sea, whipping the loose sand into the air and causing huge breakers to plunge onto the beach with a roar. Both, it must be said, have considerable appeal, especially as tests have shown that the golden sands and sparkling bathing water at Holkham are among the cleanest in the whole of Britain. Not surprisingly it attracts a large number of visitors, including the actress Gwyneth Paltrow, who was recorded walking across the sands at low tide in the closing sequence of the film *Shakespeare in Love*. If the beach is too exposed, there are firmer tracks towards the back of the dunes where the shelter-belt of pines begins.

Holkham is the largest coastal nature reserve in England, with around 1,600 acres (648 hectares) of varying coastal habitat that supports a range of wildlife. The reserve is owned by the Earl of Leicester, whose imposing family home can be visited via a short

Above: *Wells-next-the-Sea is notable for the speed of its tide, which goes out for over a mile in places and can make swimming extremely hazardous.*

excursion along Lady Ann's Road. Holkham Hall has been home to the Earls of Leicester since the 1750s and is one of Norfolk's grandest stately piles. At least half a day is really required to do justice to the house, museum and nursery, but passing coastal walkers may find the café at the entrance handily placed.

Whelks and Wet Fish at Wells

From the car park at the end of Lady Ann's Road, a boardwalk leads landwards of the trees towards Wells. The Corsican pines that make up what is known as Holkham Meals were planted in the 1860s to protect the newly reclaimed farmland from windblown sand, and reflect the pioneering agricultural and land management techniques of the Coke family of Holkham Hall. Thomas Coke, in particular, is famous as the inventor of the four-course rotation system, which revolutionized 18th-century farming. Today, the pines offer welcome protection from both the wind and the hot summer's sun.

Skirting the edge of a large caravan park you emerge at the mouth of Wells harbour, and from here walk along the top of the lofty sea wall towards the town. The bulky embankment was rebuilt following a devastating surge tide in January 1976, when the original sea wall was breached and much of the lower town was immersed. A sliding, steel floodgate was also built to seal off part of the quayside, and you can see where its rails cross the main road near the harbour office.

Wells-next-the-Sea is now the last port on the north Norfolk coast to handle commercial shipping, a place where amusement arcades and touristy craft shops mix with chandlers and boat yards. The town once boasted over a dozen granaries and maltings, but today the tall, green-painted granary that dominates the quayside has been converted into private apartments. However, the sea continues to play an important role in Wells. Whelks are still landed in sizeable quantities and, as elsewhere along the coast, there are wet-fish shops and stalls selling freshly caught lobster, crab and other shellfish. The fixed mast on the quayside outside the harbour office and Maritime Museum commemorates the disaster of 1898, when five coastguards drowned trying to reach a stricken government steam cutter offshore.

Edible Marshland?

Leave Wells by the small quayside road beyond the chandlery and when the road ends follow the signs past the sheds and boatyard. A grassy bank-top path then heads out along the edge of Warham Marsh, a vast expanse of saltmarsh that extends seawards into the distance.

Saltmarsh is formed by the build-up of mud on sheltered areas of foreshore, and because it is frequently covered by seawater only specific types of salt-resistant plants can survive. Examples include the daisy-like sea aster, sea purslane and the nationally rare shrubby seablite. In July and August the marshes are a mass of purple-blue sea lavender, and in the wetter areas you can also find marsh samphire. Also known as glasswort (because it was

---

NORFOLK'S NATIONAL NATURE RESERVES

The North Norfolk Heritage Coast boasts three exceptional National Nature Reserves (NNRs) – Scolt Head, Holkham and Blakeney Point. There are 214 NNRs in England, designated by English Nature, the government agency that champions the conservation of wildlife and geology throughout England. NNRs are designated because they are considered nationally important and are among the best examples of a particular habitat. Although wildlife comes first, most also welcome human visitors, although where the likes of nesting birds or breeding seals are particularly vulnerable (such as on the Norfolk coast), access is carefully controlled. Since all NNRs are also classed as Sites of Special Scientific Interest, it means that they enjoy a certain level of protection under the government's  wildlife legislation. The three reserves on the Norfolk coast are among the best examples in England of coastal habitat such as inter-tidal mud and sandflats, shingle ridges, sand dunes, saltmarsh and grazing marsh. Scolt Head is managed by English Nature, and Holkham by English Nature together with the Holkham Estate, while Blakeney Point is run by the National Trust. English Nature's Norfolk team produce a very useful and informative free guide to all the county's NNRs, which can either be obtained from information centres locally or from their head office at 60 Bracondale, Norwich NR1 2BE. For more general details go to www.english-nature.org.uk.

formerly used as a source of alkali for the glass industry), this succulent member of the spinach family is still harvested for the table in August, and can be eaten like asparagus or pickled in vinegar. Partly because of the sheer size of the saltmarsh and the fact that it has been kept free of human interference, this ostensibly bland-looking environment is among the most important of its kind in the whole of Europe and is a vital natural habitat.

In places, high tides can deposit a large swathe of weed across the track, and after wet weather some sections can be a little boggy, but these are not serious obstacles. Several paths and lanes lead inland to Stiffkey and Morston, where seasonal refreshment can be found; otherwise continue round to Blakeney, where there are also plenty of pubs and cafés. The handsome flint and brick buildings are typical of these picturesque Norfolk coastal villages, sitting so naturally in the landscape. In the Middle Ages, Blakeney was important for the export of wool, but like so many other ancient ports along this shore the silting of its harbour rendered it redundant – and Wells only remains open because of repeated dredging. So take your well-earned ice cream and admire the neat but modest quay, which these days hosts an array of small boats and launches offering trips to see the offshore seal colonies.

A Twitcher's Paradise

The next few miles are an ornithological treat. The coast path follows a well-walked and obvious embankment path round the edge of the marshes, with wonderful views across the creeks and pools towards the raised spit of Blakeney Point. There's usually a variety of birdlife, although what you see and where depends on the time of year. In winter, the fields echo to the honking of literally hundreds (and sometimes thousands) of geese –

Below: Stiffkey is one of a string of pretty villages on or close to the coast path, but be mindful of this particular place's pronunciation!

Brent from Russia and pink-footed from Iceland; while shelduck, oystercatcher and dunlin are all to be found beak-deep in the mud. On my last visit I was lucky enough to see a marsh harrier gliding across the marshes, and later a barn owl out in search of an early tea. In the summer, nesting lapwing and redshank, and ducks such as gadwall and shoveler, can all be found on the grazing marshes. Dotted all about are hides and observation platforms, and it is not unusual to see small groups of 'twitchers' peering excitedly through high-powered lenses at a rare migrant blown off course.

Before long, the sea bank swings inland to reach Cley next the Sea. Cley is locally pronounced 'kly', just as, further along the coast, Happisburgh is pronounced 'Aysburr' and Sea Palling 'Sea Pauling'. Also, nearby Stiffkey still sometimes comes out as 'Stukey', but the residents I spoke to mostly favoured 'Stiffkey'. If pronunciation wasn't already a veritable minefield for the hapless visitor, the local pottery (with tongue firmly in cheek) muddles matters further by calling itself Made of Cley. Also look out for the well-stocked Picnic Fayre deli, and the Three Swallows pub next to the church, which has some particularly fine photographs of old Cley and its maritime past. Cley Smokehouse, on the other hand, may require a return visit if you would like to purchase some of their mouthwatering fresh fish cured and smoked on the premises, including herring, eel, mackerel, salmon and trout. Depending on the type of fish, they are carefully brined then either hung in the two large chimneys over smouldering oak shavings for a specified period (the traditional method known as 'cold smoking'), or cooked in the kiln below (the more modern approach called 'hot smoking').

Seal-spotting off Blakeney

The National Trail leaves Cley via its handsome 170-year-old windmill (now a holiday guesthouse) then heads back out towards the sea on an embankment. At the far end, where the shingle ridge deflects the channel westwards, there is a coastguard lookout, car park and seasonal café. From here you can access Blakeney Point, a 3-mile (5-km) sand and shingle spit incorporating dunes formed by windblown sand subsequently stabilized by vegetation. It's been managed by the National Trust since 1912 and access is free, but the far western end is out of bounds between April and August to protect breeding birds and Blakeney's famous seals. Both common and grey types can be seen during spring and summer, when they haul themselves out onto the sands for an hour or so each day around low tide. However, the best way to see them is by boat, since it not only causes least disturbance but is safer, too – seals can get aggressive if you venture too close, especially when young pups are about.

Now the conditions underfoot change yet again, with the prospect of a long shingle bank all the way to Weybourne Hope. It forms part of the sea defence and is regularly bulldozed to counter the winter storms; the high, compacted top usually provides the best walking route. That said, you can

Below: Blakeney today is popular with small watercraft enthusiasts, but in the Middle Ages it was an important port for the export of wool.

also walk along the shingle shore (which does get quite arduous after a while) or better still follow a firmer strip of ground landwards of the shingle bank beside a fence.

The shingle section finishes at Weybourne Hope, where, according to the old rhyme, 'He who would old England win, must at Weybourne Hope begin'. Although the rhyme's precise origins are unclear, this is almost certainly a reference to the deep water off the Hope that allows large boats to anchor close inshore. Over the centuries it has led to fears that enemies – from the Spanish Armada through to Nazi submarines – would use the location to mount an invasion. None ever materialized, but all along this coast you will see the remains of concrete bunkers and former military lookout posts.

Crumbling Cliffs

For the rest of the way, low undulating cliffs take over. The springy turf along the top is easy and pleasant to walk, although signs remind you not to stray too near the edge. Norfolk's unstable cliffs are notoriously susceptible to erosion, and all the way along you can see where whole chunks have peeled off. However, it does allow for a close-up lesson in local geology, showing that the base chalk is overlaid with younger deposits of sands and gravels. This low but hilly landscape, known by geologists as the Cromer Forest Bed, is basically a moraine created in the last ice age and has yielded some fascinating finds, including bones, antlers and teeth of large and, in some cases, extinct animals. The remains of elephant, rhinoceros, hippopotamus and hyena have all been unearthed, suggesting that this part of Norfolk perhaps once had a milder climate than it does today.

The final stretch, alongside the golf course, contains a gentle sting in the tail – after all those miles of flatness, at last a hill! However, the trek up to the National Coastwatch Institution's lookout station (see page 37 for more details of this organization) is really very modest, and there are lovely views back along the shore towards Weybourne and a distant Blakeney Point. A shrill whistle and puffs of smoke inland will alert you to the presence of the North Norfolk Railway, the preserved steam railway known as the Poppy Line that runs between Sheringham and Holt. With the modern lifeboat station below, the path drops gently down to Sheringham's pleasant promenade, with its beach huts and benches, and a refreshing pot of tea in one of the many cafés.

The official National Trail continues for a further 5 miles (8km) from Sheringham to Cromer, but since the official route loops inland to do so, you will have undoubtedly already sampled the best the Norfolk coast has to offer.

Above: *The Poppy Line, or North Norfolk Railway, led to the development of Sheringham as a popular Victorian resort.*

Opposite: *The 170-year-old windmill at Cley next the Sea is a well-known local landmark. It operated as a mill until 1919, but has since been converted into a holiday home.*

NORTH YORKSHIRE

N orth Yorkshire's coastline is high and rugged, where huge dark
cliffs of shale are punctuated by glorious bays and coves, sometimes
sandy and welcoming, at other times harsh and rocky with wave-
cut platforms. It's a stimulating shoreline, full of interest, and one where the
human hand has played a significant part in its development – from former
whaling ports to abandoned jet and alum mines, from classic seaside resorts
to smugglers' haunts. The unstable and revealing cliffs provide fossil-hunters
and geologists with plenty of interest, while binoculars will either be trained
on the bird-rich rock faces or the busy shipping lanes.

Northern Rock

When people think of Yorkshire they tend to conjure up images of the Yorkshire Dales and North York Moors, and the high Pennine backbone dividing northern England down the middle. However, 'God's Own County' is also blessed with an impressive coastline, where old-fashioned tourist resorts such as Scarborough and Bridlington mingle with traditional fishing ports and villages like Whitby and Robin Hood's Bay.

Linking the entire coast is a long-distance footpath known as the Cleveland Way. The second-oldest National Trail in England, it runs from Filey, north of Bridlington, to Saltburn-by-the-Sea approaching Redcar. Here it heads inland for a loop round the edge of the North York Moors to Helmsley, and so completes a splendidly varied 110-mile (177-km) tour of both the coast and moors. The section described here is from Scarborough to Staithes via Robin Hood's Bay and Whitby; but the more energetic may consider extending it at either end, which will bring the total distance to around 50 miles (80km).

Right: The crowds on Scarborough's North Bay, a popular holiday seaside destination, are soon left behind once the cliff path begins.

Tourist Mecca

Scarborough is one of the classic English seaside resorts, a big and bustling town overlooking two popular sandy bays, where deckchairs, crazy golf, open-top buses and ice creams are the order of the day. The two beaches are separated by a bulky headland, topped with the remains of an 800-year-old castle, besieged six times

NORTH YORKSHIRE

Start: *Scarborough*

Finish: *Staithes*

Distance: *32 miles/51.5km*

Time: *16 hours/3 days*

Terrain: *High-level cliff paths, sometimes slippery when wet, with occasional steep flights of steps; plus beach and promenade sections.*

Ordnance Survey map: *Outdoor Leisure 27 North York Moors: Eastern Area.*

Guidebook: Cleveland Way National

Trail Guide *by Ian Sampson (Aurum Press);* Cleveland Way Information & Accommodation Guide *(free annual guide available from information centres).*

Public transport: *A free booklet of bus timetables is available locally, with services connecting to all the principal coastal centres, or go to www.yorkshiretravel.net.*

Information: *Scarborough Tourist Information Centre (01723 373333), Whitby (01947 602674); www.discoveryorkshirecoast.com; www.clevelandway.gov.uk.*

Previous pages: Former fishermen's cottages crowd around Staithes harbour.

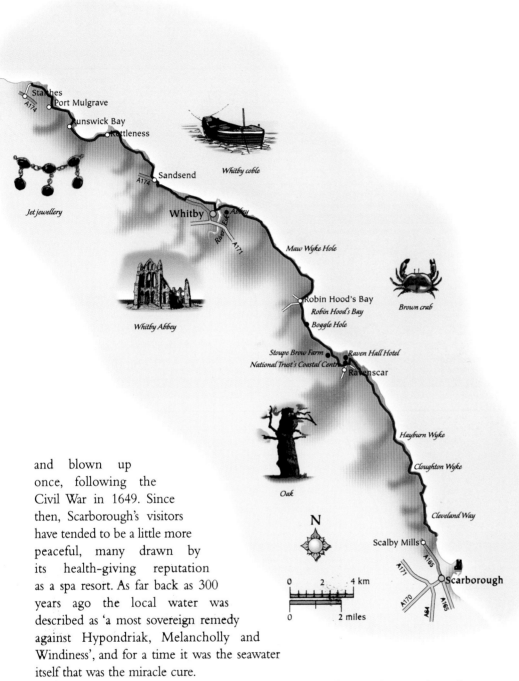

Staithes
Port Mulgrave
A174
unswick Bay
Rottleness

Whitby coble

Sandsend
A174

Jet jewellery

Whitby — Abbey

River Esk A171

Maw Wyke Hole

Whitby Abbey

Robin Hood's Bay
Robin Hood's Bay
Boggle Hole

Brown crab

Stoupe Brow Farm — *Raven Hall Hotel*
National Trust's Coastal Centre
Ravenscar

Hayburn Wyke

Cloughton Wyke

Oak

Cleveland Way

N

Scalby Mills

A171 A165

0   2   4 km

0   2 miles

A165
Scarborough
A170 A64

and blown up
once, following the
Civil War in 1649. Since
then, Scarborough's visitors
have tended to be a little more
peaceful, many drawn by
its health-giving reputation
as a spa resort. As far back as 300
years ago the local water was
described as 'a most sovereign remedy
against Hypondriak, Melancholly and
Windiness', and for a time it was the seawater
itself that was the miracle cure.

The walk begins at the northern end of Scarborough's North Bay, where the promenade
finishes by the Sea Life Centre approaching Scalby Mills. There are fine views back across the
bay: the upper slopes lined with elegant old guesthouses and the rather haunting outline of the
ruined clifftop battlement jutting out to sea. As soon as you cross the footbridge by the mill-
turned-pub and climb the steps onto the low cliffs, you lose Scarborough. The castle may still
be in sight for some miles, and there will probably be a residue of the more ambitious (or fitter)
tourists for a while, but otherwise the cliff path heads north into quiet and unfussy countryside.
The well-walked route bounds on between flat, mostly arable fields and the grassy cliff edge.
There are a few farms in sight, but as the cliffs grow higher the pleasant sense of isolation grows.

Above: The large sweep of Robin Hood's Bay, as seen from the south, where the National Trust's Coastal Centre at Ravenscar explains the history and geology of this fascinating shoreline. With the tide out, the bay's 'scars' of Jurassic rock can be clearly seen and fossils are often found.

Along the way there are old coastguard lookouts, one now housing an observation post for local ornithologists; slight route diversions are occasionally necessary where the cliffs have eroded away. This is an ongoing problem, not just along the Cleveland Way, but for most of England's east coast. Often it is only a few chunks of farmland that slip into the water, but it can be quite spectacular. Towards the end of this walk you will pass the site of the village of Kettleness, which was entirely eaten up one night in 1829; and more recently, in 1993, the Holbeck Hall Hotel on Scarborough's South Bay tumbled unceremoniously into the waves as the cliff disintegrated before its startled owners. It goes without saying that, as fascinating as it may be, walkers should keep well away from unstable cliff edges and follow official diversions.

The Resort that Never Was

The open clifftop route is interrupted at the National Trust-owned Hayburn Wyke. A 'wyke' is a wooded coastal ravine, and here at Hayburn it provides a lovely sheltered interlude, with the path wandering amid gnarled old oaks, ash and hazel, as well as ferns, mosses and rushes, all flourishing in the cool and damp conditions. Steep wooden steps bring you back out onto the clifftop, and before long a broad undercliff develops seawards, where the land appears to have slumped long ago.

Finally, the disparate buildings of Ravenscar come into view, including welcome signs for a tearoom (the Raven Hall Hotel, a little further on, also welcomes non-residents). The name of Ravenscar might come from invading Danes of the third century, who, according to the sagas, bore the image of a raven on their standards. In the 1890s developers planned a new town on this prime clifftop site, 600 feet (183 metres) above the southern end of Robin Hood's Bay. They envisaged a brand new resort to rival Scarborough, and hundreds of building plots were laid out, including sewers, water mains and roads. But although a few villas were built, the anticipated crowds of buyers never materialized, with people apparently put off by the weather and steep cliffs. Ravenscar became the town that never was.

Discovering 'The Bay'

After a short diversion inland around the Raven Hall Hotel, the Cleveland Way returns to the coast via the National Trust's Coastal Centre (open daily, April–October), where you can learn more about the Ravenscar estate. Ahead are glorious views of Robin Hood's Bay, a giant rocky sweep with the village in sight on the far side. For a while the gently sloping path above the fields runs parallel with the former Scarborough–Whitby railway line, abandoned not just because of falling passenger numbers but also because of frequent land slippage. It's now a self-styled Rail Trail, and forms part of the National Cycle Network Route One.

Below Stoupe Brow Farm, the route emerges almost onto the rocky beach by the mouth of a small stream. If the tide is low or falling you can walk the shore all the way to Robin Hood's Bay from here, which will eliminate quite a few steep steps, it must be said – but if in any doubt, stick to the path. Further on the route dips down to Boggle Hole, with the former mill turned youth hostel nestling quietly in the tree-covered valley; now it's just a short distance into the village of Robin Hood's Bay.

A LESSON IN GEOLOGY

The Yorkshire coast provides a fascinating study for geologists and fossil-hunters, with its huge cliffs of predominantly sandstone and shale created around 190 million years ago in the Jurassic period. At that point the tropical sea supported a multitude of tiny creatures, and it is the remains of these that you can find today – the ammonites, bivalves and crinoids – if you look carefully among the rock  debris at the back of the bays. Collect only a small number of fossils and make sure not to dislodge any stones from the actual cliffs, because – as will be all too clear – the soft shales and the glacial boulder clay make the cliffs extremely unstable. Elsewhere, the sheer size of the rock face reveals different bands of not just hardness but also colour. For instance, there are the near-black shales around Ravenscar, and the rusty orange seams of ironstone in the cliffs south of Staithes. Meanwhile, low tide at Robin Hood's Bay provides a splendid example of a wave-cut platform, with the domed rock strata worn away to reveal a series of concentric ledges or scars. Also look out for the large boulders scattered across the platform, which are glacial erratics transported here by the ice from Shap Fell in the Lake District around 10,000 years ago.

The settlement falls into two distinct parts. At the top of the hill are the larger, mainly red-brick buildings that date from Victorian times, while clinging to the cliffside further down is the original fishing village. It's a place of steep, narrow streets, where the houses appear to be built at odd angles and sometimes almost on top of each other. Traditional coble fishing boats landed local fish, crabs and lobsters at 'The Bay', and when the revenue men weren't looking all manner of illicit booty came ashore as well. It's said that smuggled goods landed at the harbour could work their way up the hillside from house to house without ever seeing the light of day.

It is a stunning location that naturally attracts plenty of visitors, not least for its fascinating geology – see the feature on page 75. A visit to the National Trust's visitor centre in the recently restored coastguard station above the slipway is highly recommended (open weekends throughout the year, daily from April–October). Robin Hood's Bay also sees its fair share of long-distance walkers, since not only does the Cleveland Way pass through, but it is also the eastern terminus for the Coast to Coast Walk. Alfred Wainwright's popular 190-mile (306-km) route begins at St Bees in Cumbria, where tradition has it that you dip your boots in the Irish Sea. Then, after traversing the Lake District, Yorkshire Dales and North York Moors, you finish by walking into the North Sea at Robin Hood's Bay. And, as I experienced one weary May afternoon, if the tide is low you may have to walk some way to reach it. Mind you, the pint at the Bay Hotel afterwards never tasted better.

Whitby's Maritime Past

To resume the path north of Robin Hood's Bay, you have to follow the road steeply out of the old village and turn right beyond the post office stores. Ahead is another high and exposed clifftop section, where the dazzling white plumage of the wheeling seabirds stands out against the dark, sombre cliffs. At Maw Wyke Hole,

Left: *Gazing down on the harbour for over 1300 years, Dark Age Whitby Abbey was originally founded by St Hilda and has been called the cradle of northern Christianity.*

the Coast to Coast Walk, which has been sharing your route, heads inland towards the moors, while you continue on past the lighthouse and fog signal and through a caravan park to reach Whitby Abbey.

St Hilda founded the original abbey in AD 657 and presided over the famous Synod of Whitby that decided the system for dating Easter. Although the building is now just a hollow shell, you can learn much about the abbey from the user-friendly English Heritage interpretation centre next door. Plans are also afoot to turn the historic Abbey House into a youth hostel, since the YHA currently runs the excellent cafeteria and has a small hostel nearby. From the abbey there are spectacular views over Whitby itself, with the town attractively nestled around the large natural harbour on the mouth of the River Esk. As you descend the famous 99 steps past the Church of St Mary, the roofs of the old town spread out below you. Make sure to put aside some time to explore: from the gemshops selling the local polished jet jewellery, to the fish market and restaurants like Magpie Café with its locally caught crab and award-winning fish and chips. And because Bram Stoker wrote his famous, blood-curdling novel in Whitby, don't overlook the so-called Dracula Experience on Marine Parade, whose special effects include what it calls 'live actors'.

Whitby was once the country's premier whaling port, a fact recorded in a whalebone arch across a path on the town's West Cliff. It is said that Captain William Scoresby's boat captured over 500 whales, and this locally well-known mariner is also credited for inventing the crow's nest. Nearby is a statue of another famous seafarer, Captain James Cook, who although not actually born in Whitby, went to sea from here in 1746 as an apprentice on board a collier.

Right: *Local boy, Captain James Cook, learned his trade in Whitby and sailed from here on his historic voyages to Australia and New Zealand in the mid-1700s. Cook's ships, including the* Endeavour, *were built in Whitby's shipyards.*

Two of the ships he used on his historic voyages – the *Resolution* and *Endeavour* – were built in Whitby shipyards.

Mind you, Australia and the South Seas may seem some way off if a keen wind is blowing in from the North Sea, for now your route is along the edge of the beach past the Pavilion Theatre towards Sandsend. As the name suggests, this is a glorious 3-mile (5-km) strip of sandy beach, and if the tide is low it's a wonderful, water's-edge section in good weather. Walking the opposite way on the Cleveland Way many years ago, after a punishing, day-long hike from Saltburn, I still remember the bliss of soothing hot and sore feet by splashing barefoot through the waves into Whitby.

An alternative to the beach is at first provided by the promenade at the foot of the cliffs, but after a while you have to veer inland to skirt the golf course and follow the open pavement into Sandsend. After a refuelling stop at either the pub or one of the two cafés either side of the beck, the coast path joins the route of an old railway line through a bumpy, untidy area that represents the spoil heaps of the long-vanished alum works. At the bricked-up tunnel entrance, take the extremely steep staircase by its side to return to more field-edge paths along the clifftop. Beyond the second headland is Kettleness, where the farm buildings are the only reminder of the earlier community that vanished into the sea, and beyond is a long, stepped descent through the gorse bushes to Runswick Bay. Care is needed at the foot of the steps where the path crosses a small beck and follows the rocky edge for a short distance, as the shale can be very slippery when wet. From here it's an easy amble across the sand to the buildings on the far side, including a seasonal café and toilets. Like Robin Hood's Bay, Runswick Bay is another south-facing, bayside village, and if the sun is shining on the whitewashed walls and red pantile roofs, it almost has a touch of the Mediterranean about it. Well, almost – this is Yorkshire, after all.

Ironstone, Alum and Jet

The last section of the walk begins with a steep, surfaced path above the houses – benches are helpfully provided towards the top for those who have just had their lunch and are finding it hard-going – then a track out onto the grassy clifftop from behind the Runswick Bay Hotel. Immediately ahead is Port Mulgrave, where 200 years ago a harbour was built to export the locally mined ironstone to the Jarrow ironworks. Ironstone seams occur naturally in the rocks of both the coast and the Cleveland Hills, and for a while some of the richer bands contained sufficient iron to sustain commercial mining. Meanwhile, the local shales also gave rise to alum quarrying, a vital local industry since the 14th century, as alum was used as a fixing agent for dyes in the production of textiles, as well as in the manufacture of candles and parchment and

in the tanning of leather. After the Reformation, supplies of alum from the continent dried up, so this key ingredient was all-important for the domestic woollen industry. Whole hillsides were quarried in order to process the shale, but by the end of the 19th century most were redundant, and of the 30 that were dotted along the Yorkshire coast, only the traces of the alum works that you have passed at Ravenscar and Sandsend remain.

Perhaps the Yorkshire coast's best-known mineral is jet, very hard but easily carved and highly polished. The opaque black stone is formed from fossilized trunks of the once-ubiquitous monkey puzzle or araucaria tree, and some of the best quality jet comes from the Whitby area. Jet jewellery was once very popular, particularly during Queen Victoria's mourning for Prince Albert, when she ruled that only jet ornaments were to be worn at court.

Potash is also extracted locally, and the distinctive chimneys and works beyond Staithes represent the mine at Boulby. Further on, the cliffs rise to 666 feet (203 metres), the highest on England's eastern seaboard, but unless you want to extend the walk, they can wait for another day.

Finally, the coast path drops down as the fishing village of Staithes is revealed below, huddling in a gap between the huge cliffs. The old fishing cottages are squeezed together behind the short quayside, where the Cod and Lobster pub has had to be rebuilt three times after being damaged by the sea. Unlikely as it may seem today, in the early 1800s Staithes was the biggest fishing port on the east coast, with a fleet of 84 boats. The Heritage Museum, in the former Primitive Methodist Chapel, is worth visiting to learn more about the village. It has to be said that a busy summer's weekend is probably not the best time to sample the narrow alleyways and quiet corners of this attractive place, though your fate is unlikely to be that of artists who moved to the village in the 19th century – they were pelted with fish heads by local people if they were seen painting on Sundays.

Above: The natural harbour of Staithes may have been home to an important fishing industry for centuries, but its beauty and tranquillity have also attracted writers and artists.

NORTHUMBERLAND

Deserted sandy beaches and imposing castles characterize the Northumberland coast. It's a low and open shoreline of unblemished golden strips and gentle, yawning bays. There's a scattering of fishing villages, some generally low-key tourism and, of course, a succession of impressive fortifications in various stages of repair ~ but despite its obvious beauty, this is a coast that always seems to have space aplenty. There may be queues for the causeway to Holy Island, and the master fryer at the fish and chip shop in Seahouses can be working up a sweat, but out on the beaches you can usually walk in space and freedom, enjoying the stunning seascapes and rich variety of wildlife.

A Coast of Castles

Walking Northumberland's coastline is relatively easy and straightforward. There are few real cliffs, and if the tide is favourable you can wander the open sand for long stretches, so long as you take care at the occasional river mouth and heed notices to avoid sensitive wildlife locations. Because there is so much superb beach walking to be had along these shores, it is worth checking out the tides in advance so you can time your visit to make the most of the golden sands. For local tide tables contact the nearest tourist information centre or go to the UK Hydrographic Office's on-line tidal prediction service at www.ukho.gov.uk/easytide.html.

If the tide is high or the wind is uncomfortably keen, there are alternative paths and lanes inland, and south of Embleton Bay public rights of way run along the entire coastline to Alnmouth. Although there's no set coastal trail, as such, the route is clear and well used, and with good public transport links there's ample scope for rewarding linear walks. Indeed, the Coastal Clipper open-top bus serves all the main points on the walk during summer weekends, so you can travel in style.

Right: Herring continues to be hung in the smokehouse at Craster, from where the famous kippers are exported far and wide.

The Cradle of English Christianity

Your Northumbrian coastal adventure begins at the delightful village of Bamburgh, about 20 miles (32km) south of Berwick-upon-Tweed, but try to put aside an extra day to visit the nearby Holy Island of Lindisfarne. Famous as the cradle of English Christianity, nothing survives from St Aidan's original priory, founded in AD 635 but destroyed two centuries later by uninvited guests from Denmark. The site is also associated with Cuthbert who, when his body was found miraculously undecayed 11 years after his death, turned Lindisfarne into a place of pilgrimage. The remains of a later Benedictine

Previous pages: Although Bamburgh Castle has been rebuilt many times, few such coastal defences can enjoy such an imposing position.

NORTHUMBERLAND

Start: *Bamburgh*

Finish: *Amble*

Distance: *27 miles/43km*

Time: *11 hours/2 days*

Terrain: *Easy sandy beaches, plus paths through dunes and along rocky foreshore.*

Ordnance Survey maps: *Explorer 332 Alnwick & Amble, 340 Holy Island & Bamburgh.*

Guidebook: *Northumbrian Coastline by Ian Smith (Sandhill Press).*

Public transport: *Coastal Clipper service covers entire route over summer weekends, and see local timetables for other regular coastal services: www.arriva.co.uk.*

Information: *Seahouses Tourist Information Centre (01665 720884), Craster (01665 576007), Amble (01665 712313); www.northumberland-coast.co.uk.*

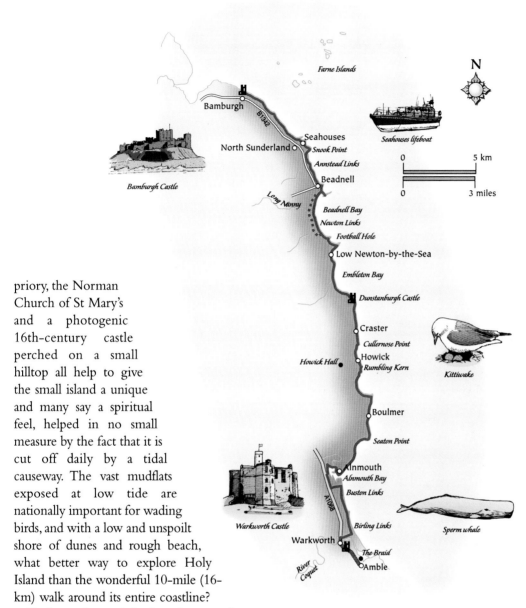

Bamburgh

Bamburgh Castle

Seahouses

North Sunderland
Snook Point

Seahouses lifeboat

Annstead Links

Beadnell

Long Nanny

Beadnell Bay
Newton Links
Football Hole

Low Newton-by-the-Sea

Embleton Bay

Dunstanburgh Castle

Craster
Cullernose Point
Howick
Rumbling Kern

Howick Hall

Kittiwake

Boulmer

Seaton Point

Farne Islands

Alnmouth
Alnmouth Bay

Buston Links

Sperm whale

Warkworth Castle

Birling Links

Warkworth

The Braid

River Coquet

Amble

priory, the Norman Church of St Mary's and a photogenic 16th-century castle perched on a small hilltop all help to give the small island a unique and many say a spiritual feel, helped in no small measure by the fact that it is cut off daily by a tidal causeway. The vast mudflats exposed at low tide are nationally important for wading birds, and with a low and unspoilt shore of dunes and rough beach, what better way to explore Holy Island than the wonderful 10-mile (16-km) walk around its entire coastline?

Back to the mainland and to another eye-catching fortification. Bamburgh Castle not so much overlooks the pretty coastal village as dominates it. Ida, King of Northumberland, was the first to make use of the handy defensive opportunities provided by this rocky outcrop, building a wooden structure in AD 547. A Norman castle followed, but over the succeeding centuries it was knocked down and patched up many times, and little remains in cohesive form from any early period. That said, it's still a fine-looking castle, and it must be difficult for visiting cricketers on the pitch below the imposing main walls to keep their eyes on the game.

The Lure of the Farne Islands

The easy, obvious and delightful way to reach Seahouses from Bamburgh is simply to walk along the broad ribbon of golden sand that stretches southwards seemingly without end. On a warm summer's day the temptation is to splash barefoot along the water's edge, but at this early stage in the day progress will inevitably be hampered and sooner or later you will have to dry damp and sandy feet. Perhaps this treat should be left until later on.

As you head along the beach you will notice a cluster of tiny islands about a mile or so offshore. These are the Farne Islands, and they represent the easternmost outcrop of the Whin Sill, a striking basalt ridge that extends intermittently across much of northern England. This volcanic rock, known as dolerite, is particularly tough and resistant to weathering, and it stands out in the landscape as high and solid dark cliffs. It was used to great advantage by the Romans who built some of Hadrian's Wall along its dark crags, but here on the coast it forms the foundations for Bamburgh Castle, as well as Dunstanburgh, which you'll visit a little later on in the walk. Offshore, the Whin Sill has created a patchwork of islets and dark reefs, and in years gone by they have proved deadly for passing ships. One of their victims was the steamer *Forfarshire* in 1838, and the daring rescue carried out by the lighthouse keeper and his 23-year-old daughter is still celebrated today (see feature on page 86).

Most visitors to the Farne Islands come for the seabirds, with popular daily boat trips from Seahouses giving visitors a chance to get up close to a wonderful array of birds – from gannets and shearwaters through to kittiwakes and razorbills. During breeding season there are thousands (and I mean thousands) of puffins, wobbling about rather comically on the cliffside and flying around with beaks full of sand eels. Then there are huge colonies of guillemots,

Below: *Up to 28 small islands and reefs make up the Farne Islands, which are not only Britain's most famous bird sanctuary, but also home to large colonies of Grey seals. The islands can be visited daily by boat trips from Seahouses.*

crowded together on ledges where without any nest they lay their single egg, shaped like a pear so that it spins round on its narrow end and doesn't roll off.

If you land on Inner Farne when the terns are breeding you are advised to wear headgear, since the protective birds dive-bomb human visitors and have been known to draw blood. St Cuthbert, one-time Bishop of Lindisfarne, lived alone on Inner Farne in quiet contemplation and solitude for many years, with only the seals and seabirds for company. Such was his affection for the wildlife of the islands that the eider duck is still known as Cuddy's duck in these parts. But even if you opt not to land and instead go on one of the round-island cruises, there are the two lighthouses (old and new) to inspect, plus the inevitability of meeting one or two grey seals along the way.

Tickets for the Farnes are sold from a line of kiosks on Seahouses harbour, a compact little place that is often busy with fishing boats, yachts and pleasurecraft. The cafés, amusement arcade and souvenir shops give the small town a touristy feel, but you can avoid most of this by leaving the harbour on the clifftop footpath (ignore the massed ranks of caravans, if you can) around Snook Point to Annstead Links. If the tide is low, Annstead Burn is fordable, but otherwise you'll have to detour the short distance to the coast road. Beyond is more glorious beach walking south to Beadnell, a small community with two popular pubs serving good quality meals. Again, much of this is hidden if you stick to the shore, but it is worth pausing

Below: The glorious sandy sweep of Beadnell Bay is backed by deep dunes, some of which are home to nesting terns in the summer.

SAVING LIVES AT SEA

The lifeboat station at Seahouses is one of 231 dotted around the coastline of the British Isles (including the Republic of Ireland) that provide a 24-hour search and rescue service, plus there are 43 'beach rescue' services located in the south-west of England. Since the Royal National Lifeboat Institution was founded in 1824, its lifeboats have saved over 136,275 lives, and in

an average year they are launched over 6,700 times and rescue as many as 6,000 people. The organization is a registered charity that depends entirely on voluntary contributions and legacies for its income, and its 4,600 lifeboat men and women are all volunteers. Such a professional but selfless service that looks after all coastal users deserves your support, so remember to make a donation when you pass the lifeboat station.

The current vessel at the Seahouses station is a Mersey Class lifeboat called the *Grace Darling*, in memory of a remarkable young woman who, together with her lighthouse-keeper father, went to the rescue of a ship that was foundering on the rocks of the Farne Islands early one stormy morning in September 1838. Together they rowed their open boat for over a mile and eventually pulled nine people to safety. Father and daughter became national heroes, and Grace was awarded the RNLI's Silver Medal for gallantry. She declined several offers of marriage in order to stay at the light, but sadly died four years later of consumption aged just 27. The RNLI's Grace Darling Museum, opposite the church at Bamburgh, commemorates her life and times and contains many of her personal belongings. For more information on the organization, go to www.rnli.org.uk.

Opposite: The magnificent ruins of Dunstanburgh Castle, which was once one of the largest and grandest castles in the north-east of England, can only be reached by foot, and this walk takes you directly to it.

by the tiny harbour with its preserved 18th-century limekilns, which are now in the hands of the National Trust.

Ahead is the graceful sweep of Beadnell Bay, a sublime stretch of sand backed by huge and sprawling dunes. There's a public footpath behind the dune system that takes you on a sturdy footbridge across a small river called Long Nanny, which is essential if the tide's not in your favour. This is also the best route to avoid disturbing the nesting terns, which between May and August breed on Newton Links. During this time the National Trust fence off the sensitive area, and wardens patrol the area around the clock to guard against disturbance. You can visit the specially erected viewing platform, next to their little wooden hut, by following a marked route from the back of the dunes, but please adhere to the waymarks and keep dogs on leads at all times. The colony can support as many as 1,700 Arctic terns, plus some little terns and ringed plover. It makes for a raucous but engrossing spectacle.

The Ruins of Dunstanburgh

At the far end of Beadnell Bay a path continues around two low headlands, separated by a tiny beach known rather mysteriously as Football Hole, then drops down to Newton Haven and the lovely hamlet of Low Newton-by-the-Sea. Here, by an immaculate square of whitewashed cottages, is the alluring Ship Inn, particularly well sited to quench the thirst of dry-throated walkers.

Above: Alnmouth, with its beautiful beach and rich history, makes for a pleasant stop on the coastal walk, but the wide and fast-flowing River Aln entails a diversion inland.

The low-tide route across the beach continues around to Embleton Bay and almost a mile and half of smooth sand that ends with a series of rocky ledges and large boulders. Join the path that has been shadowing the beach via the links golf course behind the dunes, and follow this ahead and beneath the ruins of Dunstanburgh Castle. Defences were begun in the 1300s, and for a while it was held by John of Gaunt for the House of Lancaster and played a brief but important role during the Wars of the Roses. But the castle was seized by the Yorkists on two occasions and was severely damaged by artillery, and after changing hands several times it fell into serious disrepair. By 1550 it was described as ruinous, which makes it even more remarkable that 500 or so years on some of it is still standing.

Continue south to Craster, a fishing village once renowned for its kippers. At the beginning of last century, this modestly sized community boasted 20 boats and four herring yards, where the fish were unloaded, split and gutted, then either packed in barrels of salt for export to Germany and Russia, or smoked ready for sending off to Billingsgate Market in London. Smoking traditionally takes place between June and September, when the fish are plump and their oil content is high, and involves the herring being hung over fires of oak sawdust for 10–14 hours to produce the distinctive reddish-brown kipper. The yard run by L. Robsons and Sons (dating from 1856) still survives, and oak-smoked salmon as well as kippers are on sale in the smokehouse shop, or can be sampled in the next-door restaurant.

Sea Kings and Stranded Whales

The coast path continues southwards along the low clifftop, passing the bathing house at Cullernose Point which was built by the 2nd Earl Grey of nearby Howick Hall for his family's seaside outings – since he had 16 children, these were serious undertakings. A little further on is the Rumbling Kern, a prominent hole in the rocks through which the sea periodically surges and foams.

Continue along this easy route via several lovely bays and, at low tide at least, a large area of flat, rocky ledges and pools, until you arrive at Boulmer. The yellow Sea King helicopters you may have already seen flying overhead are based at RAF Boulmer and are used in rescue operations along the coast and the hills inland.

Your route soon swings south-westwards to Alnmouth via the rock platforms of Seaton

Point. In 1973, the body of a sperm whale weighing 53 tonnes was washed ashore at this location, and after only a day or so the fermenting gases in its stomach were producing a smell so awful that the residents of Boulmer began to complain. The authorities decided that the quickest way to dispose of the huge mammal would be to blow it up, but this failed in a messy and unsatisfactory fashion, and eventually the whale's remains were chopped into pieces and buried in a huge hole in a nearby field.

A Pleasant Amble

Although there are public footpaths alongside the golf course on Alnmouth Common, the more obvious route into Alnmouth is along the broad sandy sweep of Alnmouth Bay. The small resort of Alnmouth exudes an air of respectability, with tall and elegant Victorian houses neatly laid out. However, on 23 September 1779, the calm was rudely shattered by American privateer John Paul Jones, who, in a gesture of support for the American War of Independence, fired a cannonball at the defenceless town from his ship offshore. It missed the church, thought to be its intended target, landed in a field, bounced a few times and ended up in a farmhouse roof.

A few years later, the church wasn't so lucky. In 1806 it was partly wrecked by a ferocious storm that forced the river to change direction and marooned what was left of the Norman building. Today, Church Hill stands forlornly on the southern side of the River Aln, which at low tide can be forded for about 1½ hours. However, the Aln is a serious river, and signs warn against swimming 'or even paddling' in the river estuary due to the dangerous currents, so the safest option is to detour a little inland if you want to continue to Warkworth and Amble.

From Alnmouth, follow the riverside path to cross at the road bridge, then turn off left on the cycle route that runs parallel with the A1068, and return to the shore via the lane to Buston Links. This is another enormous stretch of dune-backed beach, often largely deserted, but with the impassable mouth of the River Coquet ahead make sure to turn inland beyond Birling Links for the bridleway into Warkworth.

Sitting in a tight loop of the Coquet, the centrepiece of this ancient and attractive settlement is Warkworth Castle, or at least the surviving eight-towered keep that perches on a mound above the houses. Formerly the stronghold of the powerful Percy family, Earls of Northumberland, it is perhaps best known as the home of Harry Hotspur in Shakespeare's *Henry IV*.

To return to the coast, and the end of the walk, follow the pavement of the riverside road out towards Amble, turning off for a grassy track via an open park and picnic area known as the Braid. This was once the site of shipbuilding, since Amble was originally an industrial settlement, exporting coal from its own pit and housing a fishing fleet. Today, the harbour is mostly used by leisure craft, and beyond the Braid is Amble's modern marina, opened in 1987 and providing berths for over 200 boats.

If you've got the taste for this coast and want to continue the walk southwards there's another lovely bay just a mile or so further on at Druridge. With over 6 miles (10km) of continuous sandy beach, and backed by Hauxley and East Chevington nature reserves, it's easy to see why the Northumbrian coast is up there with the best.

Below: *Dolerite boulders are strewn across the Northumbrian shore near Embleton.*

FIFE

'A fringe of gold on a beggar's mantle' was how James II of Scotland described the East Neuk of Fife, a mostly low coastal strip of picturesque fishing towns based on a series of sheltered bays. 'Neuk' is the old Scots word for corner, and the historical importance of the small peninsula is reflected in the fact that many of the small towns are royal burghs. Each retains its own distinctive character, and no more so than in the splendid architecture that will leave you fascinated and awed in equal measure.

The Kingdom of Fife

The Fife Coastal Path extends 81 miles (130km) around the entire peninsula, joining the Forth railway bridge at North Queensferry with the Tay road bridge at Newport, and the walk featured here focuses on the section through the East Neuk. With the exception of St Andrews, the communities are small and unpretentious, and perfectly complement the gentle and unspoilt nature of this coastal route. Indeed, beyond Crail and Fife Ness the route is quite wild and comparatively little walked, and because there are one or two sections where the route is still being finalized you are required to follow the foreshore for short periods. Overall the route is efficiently waymarked, and there are even signs guiding you through the built-up areas along the way. Mind you, it's quite likely that you'll end up finding your own way around the charming streets of Elie, Pittenweem, Anstruther and Crail, since the Kingdom of Fife has a charm that takes hold before you know it.

Right: *Fresh crabs and lobster continue to be landed regularly at Anstruther, home of the Scottish Fisheries Museum.*

Around Largo Bay

Leven sits at the far western side of Largo Bay, wide and curving, and it's at Leven Links at the eastern edge of the town that you begin the walk. By the car park next to the holiday village is the first of what will be a succession of informative noticeboards showing a map, distance breakdown and background details to each chunk of the coast path. As you will see, the first stage is straightforward, either following the sandy beach or if the tide is high a path behind the caravans and then through the dunes. Ahead, the scene is dominated by Largo Law, modest in height (951 feet/290 metres) but splendidly volcanic in shape. Out in the Forth estuary you might see the giant rigs, which are constructed in a special yard along the coast at Methil, being towed out to the oil fields of the North Sea.

After crossing the first of what will be numerous

Previous pages: *Anstruther is the largest village along the East Fife shore and, although fishing isn't the industry it once was here, the harbour is still a vibrant place.*

FIFE

Start: *Leven*

Finish: *St Andrews*

Distance: *33 miles/53km*

Time: *15 hours/2–3 days*

Terrain: *Sandy bays and straightforward, grassy cliff paths, but much wilder after Crail with sections of rough foreshore.*

Ordnance Survey maps: *Explorer 370 Glenrothes North, 371 St Andrew's & East Fife.*

Guidebook: *Fife Coastal Path official guide.*

Public transport: *There are excellent bus links between all the main coastal centres, so pick up a copy of Fife Council's Getting Around Fife locally or go to www.fifedirect.org.uk.*

Information: *Anstruther Tourist Information Centre (01333 311073), Crail (01333 450869), St Andrew's (01334 472021); Fife Coastal Path Information Desk (01592 414300); www.fifecoastalpath.co.uk.*

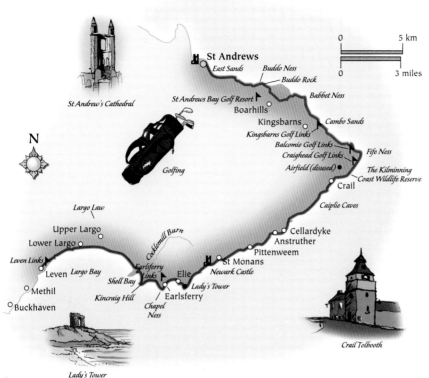

St Andrews
East Sands — Buddo Ness
— Buddo Rock
Babbet Ness
St Andrew's Cathedral
St Andrews Bay Golf Resort
Boarhills
Kingsbarns — Cambo Sands
Kingsbarns Golf Links
Balcomie Golf Links —
Craighead Golf Links — Fife Ness
Airfield (disused) — The Kilminning Coast Wildlife Reserve
Golfing
Crail
Caiplie Caves
Largo Law
Upper Largo
Lower Largo — Cellardyke
Anstruther
Cocklemill Burn
Pittenweem
Leven Links — St Monans
Leven — Largo Bay — Earlsferry Links — Newark Castle
Methil — Shell Bay — Elie
Buckhaven — Kincraig Hill — Lady's Tower
— Earlsferry
Chapel Ness

Crail Tolbooth

Lady's Tower

golf courses, the route reaches Lower Largo. Continue along the main street past the small harbour, and if the name of the waterside Crusoe Hotel leaves you puzzled, all is explained a little further on by a small statue above the doorway of a terraced house. It celebrates the life and times of Alexander Selkirk, born here in 1676, who achieved fame after spending four years marooned on a deserted Pacific island. The novelist Daniel Defoe was so taken with his story that it inspired him to write *Robinson Crusoe*, based on Selkirk's life.

Behind Temple car park, the route takes to the course of an old railway, then heads out across Dumbarnie Links Nature Reserve, important for its vast and untouched dune system. Summer-flowering purple milk-vetch, meadow cranesbill, common and greater knapweed and viper's bugloss support a range of butterflies and insects.

After fording Cocklemill Burn, follow the shoreline around to Shell Bay, but, if the tide is high, you will have to divert inland to the footbridge and then follow the waymarks through the sprawling caravan park. Ahead is an ascent of what is arguably the one proper cliff on the whole of the route. Mind you, the track up onto Kincraig Hill is easy enough, and from the top there are great views across the Forth to Bass Rock and the distant Pentland Hills beyond Edinburgh. Leven can be pinpointed by the pencil-thin tower of Methil power station behind. The grassy hilltop is nowadays home to various modern transmitters and masts, while the dilapidated concrete buildings and decayed fencing is testimony to the radar station and battery that was positioned here during the Second World War.

For the seriously intrepid there is another way of approaching Kincraig Point. This is via the famous chain path below the cliffs, where long links of tough chain have been fastened to the steeply sloping rock and – like the Via Ferrata routes in the Italian Alps – ambitious types can scramble and haul themselves along above the waves. It's a strenuous and challenging route, and not for the faint-hearted. I'm quite happy to admit that I left it for another day.

Shrines and Salt at St Monans

Drop down to the back of West Bay and skirt the links before rounding Chapel Ness to enter the joined-up villages of Earlsferry and Elie (the latter is pronounced 'Eelee'). Earlsferry marks the old crossing point across the Forth to North Berwick, the latter indicated across the water (weather permitting) by the distinctive, lumpy outline of Berwick Law. The coast path trots along the neat and respectable main street of Elie and out onto the low clifftop towards St Monans. Make sure to visit the small lighthouse on Elie Ness and Lady's Tower just beyond. This partly restored stone tower was built for Lady Jane Anstruther by her husband in the late 1700s. She used it as a bathing house, for her ladyship liked nothing better than to swim naked in the sea, and when she headed for the tower a bell was rung around Elie to warn the townspeople to stay away.

Below: Lower Largo, near Leven, overlooks the wide sweep of Largo Bay. It was here that Alexander Selkirk, the inspiration for Robinson Crusoe, was born.

Further along the cliffs you come to the ruins of the 16th-century Newark Castle. At the time of writing the crumbling remains are fenced off, with a sign explaining that a current archaeological dig is a likely prelude to restoration. Nearby is a doocot (dovecot) that dates from the same period. Continue into St Monans on a path that follows a rocky ledge below the church (there's an inland alternative if the tide is high).

The town is named after the Irish missionary St Monan, who was slain during a Danish raid in AD 874. A local shrine, said to contain his relics, became famous for its healing powers, and one of its grateful visitors was King David II (1329–71), who had been injured in battle. Upon recovery, he had the shoreside church built as a mark of gratitude. Follow the signs through the town, past the slipway still occasionally used by local boat-builders, and on via the harbour.

On the eastern edge of the town you pass a restored windmill that was built in the 1770s to facilitate salt production, pumping seawater into giant pans where it was evaporated by coal-burning furnaces to leave just the crystals. Salt was at one time the most important Scottish export after wool and fish, but with growing competition from English rock salt and purer sea salt from southern Europe the industry declined, and

national production finally ceased at Prestonpans in 1959. Here, at St Monans, the nine salt pans remain well preserved, and the windmill itself is open during the summer (the key is available locally at other times).

The Royal Burghs of Anstruther

The beauty of this section of the coast path is that not only is it well waymarked and generally uncomplicated to follow, but it is also relatively flat and easy to walk, since it follows a raised beach for most of the way. And, as you will find, there's a rapid succession of fascinating and picturesque towns. The next is Pittenweem, whose name means place (or pit) by the cave (*weem*). The cave in question is where St Fillan lived while he was busy converting the Picts to Christianity; incorporating a well and altar, it can still be seen in the middle of the town on Cove Wynd. It is said that St Fillan was able to read in the dark when a mysterious light emanated from his left arm.

Today, Pittenweem boasts the main fishing fleet of the East Neuk, and the fish market on the quayside is still a busy place most mornings. Also by the harbour is Gyles House, built in the early 1700s for a Captain James Cook, who carried Charles II to France after his defeat at the Battle of Worcester in 1651. Like all the East Neuk coastal settlements, Pittenweem's historic buildings are full of colour and character, nowhere more so than when you enter the town via West Shore. Each whitewashed house and cottage is irresistibly unique, from the brightly painted frames of the doors and windows through to the crow-stepped gable ends. If you look closely you'll see that some of the oldest buildings have a set of initials and a date discreetly painted high up below the red pantile roofs: the traditional signature of the builder.

Above: Lady's Tower on Elie Ness was built in the 1770s as a changing room to facilitate Lady Anstruther's penchant for skinny-dipping!

Opposite: *Named after a 9th-century Irish missionary, medieval St Monan's Church stands right on the very edge of the shore of the Firth of Forth.*

Beyond Pittenweem the trail hugs the rocky shore and rounding another links course enters the larger settlement of Anstruther. In fact, Anstruther is made up of three royal burghs: Anstruther Wester, Anstruther Easter and Cellardyke. At one time each had its own harbour, but now the three communities have more or less merged. The main seafront has plenty of pubs and cafés to revive the flagging walker, plus a couple of fish and chip shops. These are particularly apposite, since next to the tourist information centre is the Scottish Fisheries Museum, which traces the development of the Scottish fishing industry over the centuries and contains a number of real boats used over the years. If fishing heritage is not high on your agenda, then it's still worth popping in to enjoy their excellent tearoom.

Follow the signs through Cellardyke, and beyond the caravan park the coast path resumes its pastoral progress seawards of fields containing very contented-looking, free-roaming pigs. The red sandstone caves at Caiplie will catch your attention, since over the centuries various people have left their marks in the soft rock – from crosses carved by medieval monks and pilgrims to names and initials of local children. The latter still try to throw stones through the small hole high up in the south-westerly cliff; it is said that if you are successful, your wish will come true.

Rounding the Ness

The last in the string of East Neuk settlements is Crail, and as you round the headland and thread your way through the cottages, its tiny but delightful harbour is revealed below. A sign advertising locally caught lobster and dressed crab indicates that shellfish is now the main catch, although this royal burgh was once famous for its dried or smoked herring, known rather misleadingly as Crail capon. A herring is depicted in the weathervane on the top of the Tolbooth further up the hill, which houses the old gaol and council offices, while on nearby Marketgate the interesting museum and heritage centre (open Easter–September) is also worth visiting.

In the 12th century King David I built a castle above the harbour, and although it is now long gone it is at least remembered in Castle Walk, a superb, high-level walkway that affords great views over the Forth to Bass Rock and the Lothian coast around North Berwick and Dunbar. Closer to hand, about 6 miles (10km) offshore, is the Isle of May, a small and rocky

Right: *The red sandstone caves at Caiplie were weathered by waves thousands of years ago to form wonderful, organic shapes.*

island that is home to thousands of nesting seabirds and a large colony of grey seals. There are daily boat trips from Anstruther, and in late spring you can be treated to the sight of as many as 50,000 pairs of nesting puffins, as well as large numbers of shags, razorbills and guillemots.

Drop down to the seafront walk and follow this out past more caravans and via The Kilminning Coast Wildlife Reserve to Fife Ness. On the way you pass the site of Crail Airfield, which has had a fascinating history. It was established in 1918 to provide grass runways for British and American fighter reconnaissance aircraft, then during the Second World War it became one of the first major Fleet Air Arm training airfields in the UK. HMS Jackdaw air torpedo

Above: *St Andrews is many things to many people; a place of pilgrimage, education and entertainment (particularly for golfers). The town is steeped in history and boasts the oldest university in Scotland, a fine cathedral and wonderful links courses.*

training was practised in the Firth of Forth by aiming at target vessels such as SS *Glen Usk*, a converted Bristol paddle steamer. After 1947 the base was recommissioned as HMS Bruce, providing training for 15-year-old boy seamen in the arts of gunnery, seamanship and communication. Then, after a short spell in the 1950s when the Black Watch was billeted at the airfield prior to departure for war in Korea, the site was used by St Andrews University Air Squadron, and finally it served as a base for the Joint Services School for Linguists. In the 1960s, the land was sold back to local farmers and the airfield buildings became derelict.

Today, this isolated corner of Fife is, walkers notwithstanding, mostly peopled by golfers on the Craighead Links, as well as coastguards in the lookout station on the tip of the Ness. The trail passes below the main building and the light, and via the wooden hide that the local bird club uses to track passing migrants.

Scotland's Patron Saint

After Fife Ness the coast path changes its complexion. Not only does it head north-west instead of north-east, but the remaining 10 miles (16km) or so to St Andrews are along a rougher and sometimes challenging shoreline. There are no more towns or villages – no facilities at all, in fact, unless you divert to the shop and restaurant at Kingsbarns, so make sure to pack sufficient food and drink. Instead, it's a succession of golf links, open fields and occasionally foreshore. If you have allowed plenty of time and the weather is kind, this can be very pleasant, but in adverse conditions the soft sand can be arduous and the rocks slippery. And if the tide is high the route may also be temporarily blocked and you will have to sit patiently for a while before proceeding.

The golf theme continues as you skirt Balcomie and later Kingsbarns Links, and towards the end you also pass seawards of St Andrews Bay 'Golf Resort and Spa'. From Babbet Ness there are new views across to Arbroath and the coast of Angus, but after this the coast path makes a short inland diversion alongside the tree-lined Kenley Water, before returning to the coast via a farm lane south of Boarhills.

The final part of the path is narrow and in summer quite overgrown, and scampers up and down the low cliffs. On the way it passes Buddo Rock, a huge sandstone rock sculpted into wonderful shapes, with a natural staircase leading up a narrow middle passage. Although the trail is reasonably easy to follow, it will inevitably take longer than you think. Finally, the path descends to join the holidaymakers at East Sands, and the bustling, popular resort of St Andrews.

St Andrews has a long and illustrious history as a seat of religious and academic learning. Legend has it that St Regulus (or St Rule) brought the relics of Scotland's patron saint back to the remote headland of Kilrymont. St Andrew was martyred on a diagonal cross – hence the shape of the saltire embodied in the nation's blue and white flag. Only St Rules Tower remains from the original church, succeeded by a cathedral that, when finished in the 1200s, was the grandest in Scotland; and a castle that served as a palace, fortress and prison. Scotland's first university was founded at St Andrews in 1410.

Beyond St Andrews the Fife Coastal Path is forced inland around the Eden estuary and RAF Leuchars, but then enjoys the sandy miles of Tentsmuir Point before swinging west along the banks of the Firth of Tay opposite Dundee. The 'fringe of gold' is rich indeed.

SCOTLAND'S FAMOUS LINKS GOLF COURSES

With 46 separate golf courses dotted around the small peninsula and a history of playing the game stretching back to the 1400s, Fife is without doubt steeped in the sport. Many are links courses, which means they are laid out along the open coastal strip. St Andrews is the home of the Royal and Ancient club, and in 2005 the famous Old Course hosted the Open Championship for the 27th time. The town is full of golf shops, and near the clubhouse on the seafront is the British Golf Museum, where you can explore 500 years of golfing history and try your hand on a mini putting green using replica clubs and balls from the past.

The walk featured here skirts many of the finest links courses, including the new one at Kingsbarns, which hosted the Millennium Open. Others, like Earlsferry Links, have been in existence for centuries, and a plaque at the town hall celebrates local golfer James Braid who won the Open Championship five times between 1901 and 1910. Golf is part of the social fabric here – James II even banned it in 1547 because men were golfing instead of practising archery – and they play golf in Fife all year round. Where the coast path crosses a golf course you will come across noticeboards politely spelling out a code of conduct for walkers. The main points are: wait for the golfers to take their shots; keep to the path or shoreline wherever possible and avoid greens and fairways; keep noise levels down and stay alert at all times.

SANDWOOD BAY, SUTHERLAND

*A*lmost 2 miles (3km) of smooth and spotless white sand, backed by windblown rolling dunes and a dark and brooding loch with, on either side, finely chiselled rocky headlands that funnel the endlessly crashing surf: this is Sandwood Bay. Located within sight of Cape Wrath, near the extreme north-west tip of the British mainland, the bay has no beach-side café or toilet block, nor even a handy car park. Instead, to reach Sandwood's unblemished sands you have to walk almost 5 miles (8km) along a rough moorland track, longer if you come from the north. It's an experience to savour, to soak up and, for many people, it's a very special place.

The Last Wilderness

Hamish MacInnes, the knowledgeable and respected outdoor writer, describes Sandwood Bay as 'a beach fashioned in a grand scale, more magnificent than any other I have seen, even in the Southern Hemisphere'. The key to its continuing appeal lies in its remoteness and relative inaccessibility. It's not an overly difficult walk, but it does tend to cut out the casual sightseers and leaves what is probably Scotland's (and perhaps Britain's) finest beach for the people who really *want* to experience it. And what a prospect it is, with the mountain backdrop of Sutherland extending to Cranstackie and Foinaven in the far distance.

Although Sandwood may be remote it doesn't necessarily mean you will have it to yourself. During the main holiday period and over popular weekends there will be others wandering about, perhaps enjoying a picnic on the beach or occasionally camping among the dunes. One or two hardy souls even drag their surfboards all the way there to ride the relentless breakers, but swimming is not recommended due to the dangerous currents and powerful undertow. However, Sandwood is also about space, and whether you find a little niche in the dunes or a spot beside a rocky promontory on the cliffs above, there'll always be somewhere you can relax on your own and take in the magnificent surroundings.

Right: Kinlochbervie still retains a fishing fleet and a daily quayside market.

Indeed, if you choose a quiet time to visit, you can enjoy Sandwood in perfect solitude, and it is this peace and quiet and unspoilt natural beauty that is the essence of Sandwood. John Muir (see feature on page 108) is regarded as one of the founding fathers of the modern conservation movement, a man passionately committed to the preservation of wild spaces, and the charity that takes his name and which now owns and manages Sandwood is keen to protect the inherent wildness of this remote and spectacular location. To that end, dogs are not allowed at Sandwood (it is a nature conservation area with grazing stock) and you are asked to take all your litter home with you and leave no trace of your visit. In that way, generations to come can continue to enjoy the magic of Sandwood.

SANDWOOD BAY

Start/finish: Blairmore, near Kinlochbervie

Distance: 10 miles/16km

Time: 5 hours/1 day

Terrain: Clear but sometimes boggy moorland track, sandy shore and rough cliff paths.

Ordnance Survey map: Explorer 446 Durness & Cape Wrath.

Guidebook: None.

Public transport: None.

Information: Durness Tourist Information Centre (01971 511259); www.jmt.org/cons/sand/

Previous pages: The huge, deserted sweep of Sandwood Bay viewed from the south.

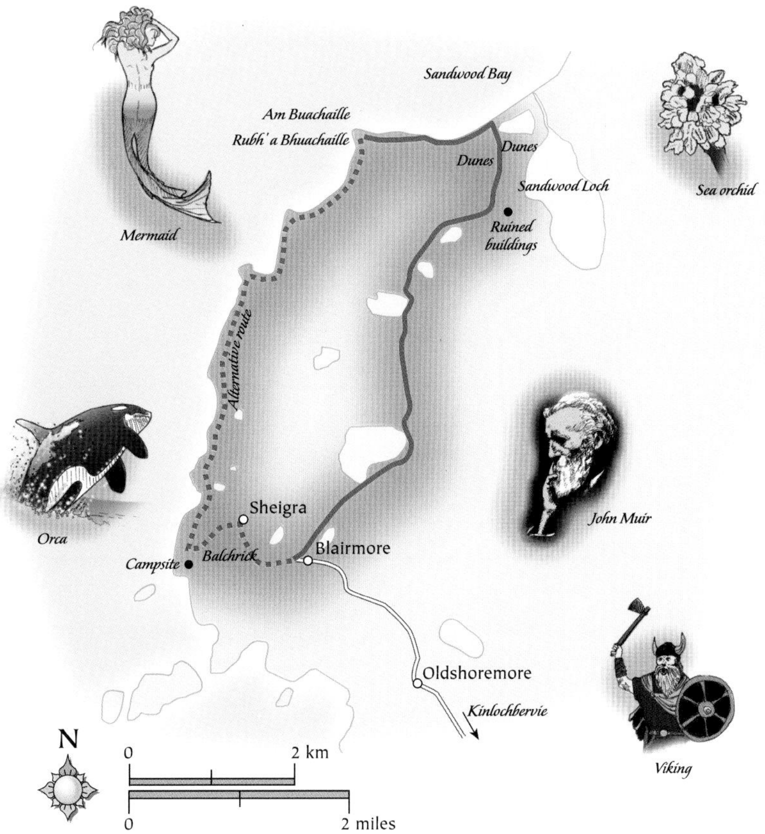
Sandwood Bay
Am Buachaille
Rubh' a Bhuachaille
Dunes
Dunes
Sandwood Loch
Ruined buildings
Sea orchid
Mermaid
Alternative route
Orca
John Muir
Sheigra
Campsite
Balchrick
Blairmore
Oldshoremore
Kinlochbervie
Viking
N
0
2 km
0
2 miles

A Moorland Approach

The walking route to the bay begins at a small car park between Blairmore and Balchrick, towards the end of the lane from Kinlochbervie. You may be surprised to learn that as recently as the 1980s, Kinlochbervie, a large village known locally as KLB, vied with Fraserburgh to be the third busiest port for white-fish landings in Scotland. The fish market still takes place at the waterfront halls at 6pm Monday to Thursday and 2pm on Fridays, and is a lively event. The nearby crofting community of Oldshoremore also boasts a superb beach of its own, and there is a secluded bayside campsite further along the lane at Sheigra.

Your journey to Sandwood begins opposite the car park and telephone box, where there is a simple sign and a gate across the track to deter vehicles. Ahead is just under 5 miles (8km) of gently undulating but unremarkable moorland walking, the first part of which is along a firm track. Later on you will see how the John Muir Trust has had to carry out counter-erosion measures such as stone pitching in an effort to reduce problems caused in the past by motor vehicles, and after wet weather this section of the path can get muddy and slippery.

Below: *A distant view of Handa Island from Balchrick.*

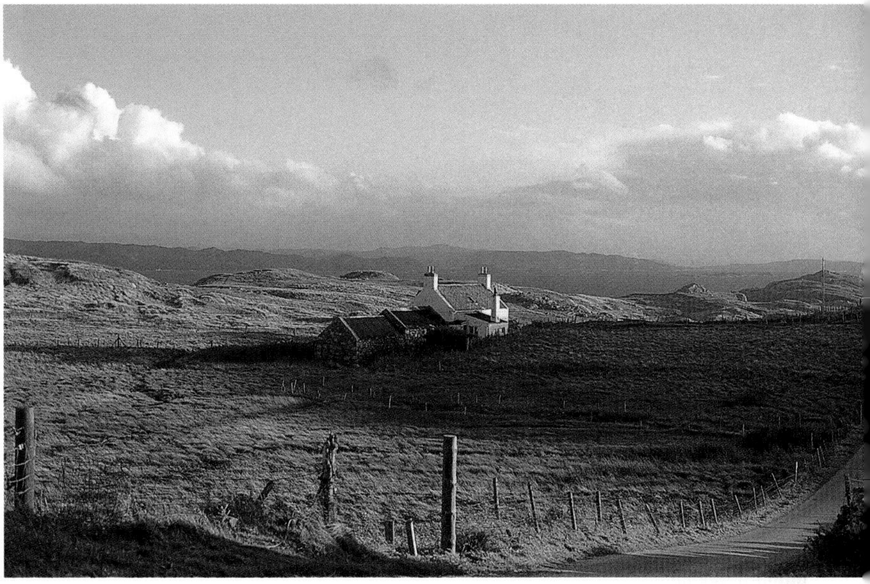

Above: *At the back of the bay is the reed-fringed Sandwood Loch, whose dark, peaty waters host ducks and other wildfowl.*

Opposite: *The impressive sea stack of Am Buachaille, over 200 feet (65 metres) high, is visible to the south of the bay.*

Before too long the bay creeps into view below. Immediately you are struck by the large freshwater expanse of Sandwood Loch reaching into the moors behind, which, like the lochans you have passed along the way, may play host to a few ducks and even the odd red-throated diver. Also look out for golden plover, greenshank and dunlin among the wet, peaty moors. Seaward of the loch is what is known in Scotland as the 'machair', a Gaelic term defining a fertile and rare coastal grassland that is usually formed by windblown sand that stabilizes over time. It's mostly found on the west coast of Scotland and among the Hebridean islands, and is especially rich in plantlife. The machair of Oldshoremore and Sheigra, for instance, has been found to host over 200 species, including at least eight different orchids. Beyond the machair at Sandwood is a sprawling dune system. Some of the dunes reach impressive heights but are notoriously unstable and prone to erosion, and careful restoration work, including the planting of native marram grass, is helping to secure this delicate area.

For most first-time visitors the highlight of Sandwood Bay is the glorious strip of sand, formed by eroded sandstone and the crushed-up remains of countless sea shells, and punctuated at low tide by two small rocky outcrops. On either side the cliffs rise up spectacularly, with plenty of bare and unstable rock for budding geologists to examine. They are mainly made up of Torridonian sandstone and conglomerate (coarse-grained sedimentary rock made up of lots of smaller pieces), with small outcrops of Lewisian gneiss. The gneiss is the oldest rock in the region – in fact, one of the oldest rocks on the planet – producing a bumpy landscape of low, undulating hills and lochans. The Torridonian sandstone produces the more angular and spectacular formations, such as sea stacks, as well as the huge domes of eye-catching mountains such as Suilven, Canisp and Quinag, many of which are topped by white Cambrian quartzite. No wonder north-west Scotland is such a fascinating and visually remarkable place.

A Place of Legends and Ghostly Sightings

Up to 300 feet (90 metres) high in some places, the rugged cliffs continue along this dramatic coast all the way north to Cape Wrath, and south via a series of spectacular rockfalls, sliding blocks and sea stacks to Sheigra. From the beach at Sandwood the impressive stack of Am Buachaille (the herdsman) is visible below the bay's southern headland of Rubh' a Bhuachaille. This 223-foot-high, pencil-like sandstone column rises from a ledge just off the foot of the cliffs, and apart from a few intrepid climbers it remains the preserve of gulls and fulmars.

There is little shelter at Sandwood if the weather is rough, so make sure to take adequate protective clothing if the forecast is uncertain. However, lively weather conditions only serve to accentuate the wildness of the location, and the sight and sound of the surf crashing on the shore is awesome. But if you do venture onto the cliffs to watch the spectacle, beware the eroded cliff edges and be mindful of the gusting wind.

At the other end of the scale, a mild and sunny summer's day at Sandwood is idyllic. On one occasion (at the end of May, no less!), I paddled in the waves below a beating sun and clear blue sky, a scene more reminiscent of the South Pacific than Sutherland. The dazzling white sand and deep blue sea was mesmeric and, until I admitted to myself that the intensely cold water was gradually turning my feet numb, it was hard to believe that this was a small beach in northern Scotland.

There are many stories and legends associated with Sandwood, although some appear more authentic than others. The Vikings are known to have visited these shores, with King Hakon anchoring his large fleet near here in 1263 prior to his invasion of the mainland. It is believed that they gave Sandwood its original name of Sandwick. Much later, in the 1840s, the small Sandwood community was turfed out to make way for a vast new sheep run let to a Kinlochbervie merchant. The residents were packed off on a boat from Loch Laxford bound for a new life in the New World.

At the back of the bay by the loch is a ruined cottage, which, rather inevitably, is supposed to be haunted. According to one account, the ghost is a bearded sailor in boots, cap and tunic, the sole survivor of an Armada galleon that was wrecked off Cape Wrath and whose treasure still lies buried in the sand. (Another version makes the ghost a stranded Polish seafarer.) Whatever his origin or nationality, apparently the old sea dog still wanders the dunes in the dark and bangs on the cottage window during stormy nights. Two walkers are said to have run terrified all the way back to civilization after encountering the spectre during a night's bivouac in the old building. There's also another tale (where do some of them come from, I wonder?) that describes the ghost of an old Australian man who, enchanted with Sandwood, visited it on numerous occasions. Although he eventually died many thousands of miles away, they say his soul made the final return trip and still resides there. Listen out, in particular, for a heavy tread…

Below: *Newly planted marram grass has helped stabilize the wind-blown dunes at Sandwood.*

Another story tells of how a local shepherd called Alexander Gunn, while looking for one of his sheep on a January day in 1900, encountered a mermaid trapped on the rocks in the middle of the beach at low tide, waiting for the sea to return. At first he thought it was seal, but looking closely he saw that she had reddish-yellow hair, greenish-blue eyes and a yellow body about 7 feet long. Until his dying day, he swore blind that the story was true. Latterly, during an exceptionally hot period one recent summer, the sightings of a modern strain of naked, 'two-legged' mermaids caused some amusement, and I suspect not a little curiosity among the male members of the local population.

Above: Sandwood Loch and the supposedly haunted ruined cottage.

A Moorland or Coastal Return

Because of the force and fetch of the sea, the beach is often littered with sea-borne debris. Local volunteers periodically clear the sand of as much of it as they can and campers tend to burn what wood they find over beach fires. As far as I know, no treasure has yet been found at Sandwood, but it wasn't too long ago that the remains of old wrecks could still be seen around the bay. In his 1935 book *Highways and Byways in the West Highlands*, author Seton Gordon told of his astonishment at finding so many wrecked vessels lying in or on the sand. It turned out that they all dated from a century or more previously – before the Cape Wrath lighthouse was built.

The straightforward return to the car park at Blairmore is back along the moorland track. If you have enjoyed your visit and want to contribute towards the upkeep of Sandwood, please drop some money in the John Muir Trust donations box near the public telephone.

However, stronger and more ambitious walkers can opt for a different return by following the clifftop southwards. It's an undulating and sometimes quite rough route, and although there is an intermittent path, you will probably end up finding your own way among the low heather, rocks and rough grass. Despite this, the impressive cliff scenery is worth the effort and, eventually, after a couple of fence stiles above Sheigra, you join the end of the lane past the campsite back to the car park at Blairmore. This return route via the coast is approximately 6 miles (10km) long.

One other option is also worth considering, so long as the weather is decent and you are fit and well equipped. Looking north from Sandwood, the lighthouse at the tip of Cape Wrath is just visible, and it is possible to follow the clifftop for the 7 or 8 miles (11–13km) to reach Britain's most north-westerly point – but beware, it is a rough journey and will invariably take longer than you think, plus you must give careful thought to your return leg.

Keeping a Watch for Wildlife

On your walk along the clifftop, keep your eyes peeled for marine life, and in particular for passing cetaceans: whales, porpoises and dolphins. The sea off Cape Wrath is a good place to see minke whales in the summer months, as well as white-beaked and Risso's dolphins. Pods of orcas (killer whales) also occasionally come close to the shore hunting for seals, and common or harbour porpoises can often be seen swimming together in small groups. Calm days are best for viewing cetaceans, and their presence is often indicated by gulls flocking above a shoal of fish. If you make a sighting, try to establish the size and shape of the dorsal fin (sickle-shaped like a dolphin or upright like an orca?), whether it jumps or bow rides like some types of dolphin or has the characteristic blow of a whale. They may be some way off land, but when you see a school of dolphins or pod of whales through your binoculars for the first time it's a thrilling moment. For more details of what to see and where to go to see them, contact the Hebridean Whales and Dolphin Trust, 88 Main Street, Tobermory, Isle of Mull PA75 6NU, tel. 01688 302859, or go to www.hwdt.org.

Cape 'Wrath' comes from the Norse *hvarf*, meaning turning point, although it's tempting to suppose that the name of this notorious meeting place of the Pentland Firth and the Minch could equally well derive from the ire of distressed mariners. A remote and lonely spot, Cape

---

THE JOHN MUIR TRUST

Sandwood Bay in Sutherland is owned and managed by the John Muir Trust, a charity set up in 1983 to protect and conserve wild places. It owns a number of key sites in Scotland, such as the mountain of Schiehallion near Loch Tummel, some of the Knoydart peninsula and a large chunk of Ben Nevis, including the summit. It also has three properties on Skye, covering the hills and coastline around Strathaird, Torrin and Sconser. The trust actively encourages local communities to become involved in the running and guardianship of these areas. At Sandwood, for instance, the estate is under crofting tenure, with around 30 crofting tenants renting an enclosed area of land (the croft) and exercising their rights to graze livestock over an adjoining area of open moorland (known as the common grazings). There are over 17,700 crofts in the Highlands and Islands of Scotland, of which the vast majority remain part of this semi-feudal tenure system that is centuries old. It's a unique social arrangement, based on small-scale agricultural production and embodying a strong sense of community. The John Muir Trust aims to reinforce this bond on the Sandwood estate by bringing crofters onto the committee that discusses issues such as estate maintenance and visitor management. A local crofter is employed as a full-time Conservation Manager, and organizes routine work such as footpath renewal and removing derelict fencing.

Another core aim of the trust is to increase the awareness and understanding of visitors to wild places, and to that end they promote the John Muir Award, a scheme that encourages people of all ages to discover and conserve wild places. The trust is named after the 19th-century naturalist and explorer John Muir, who was born in Scotland but lived most of his life in the United States, where he is recognized as the pioneer of the modern conservation movement and founder of the national park concept. His instruction was to 'do something for wildness and make the mountains glad'. To find out more about the trust's activities and how you can help, go to www.jmt.org.

Wrath is usually reached from Durness, which is east of the cape, after a ferry ride over the Kyle of Durness and a long minibus trip along a bumpy track. The journey is certainly worthwhile, for apart from the (now unmanned) lighthouse built in 1828 by Robert Stevenson, the precipitous cliffs around Cape Wrath boast vibrant seabird colonies. This is especially true to the east at Clo Mor, which at 920 feet (281 metres) represent mainland Britain's highest vertical sea cliffs. It is an amazing sight, and in the summer the ranger service organizes guided walks so you can discover more.

Standing on the open cape gazing out at the dark, choppy waters, you can feel the isolation and remoteness, a point reinforced by the fact that the next land you come to northwards is the Arctic. If the conditions are clear you may see Lewis to the south-west and the flat outline of Orkney away to the north-east, but it is also quite likely that you will struggle even to stand upright if the wind is roaring in across the treeless headland. Visitors using the minibus service to Cape Wrath should also bear in mind that an area of the north coast near the cape is an active military range, and bombing practice can hinder access – check at Durness Tourist Information Centre beforehand.

Whether your penchant is for the wild and towering cliffs of Cape Wrath, or the golden sand and sparkling waters of Sandwood Bay, this remote corner of Britain is a must for all discerning coastal lovers. It is another reminder that even in our comparatively tiny and crowded island there remain some stretches of truly wild coastline that are among the best in the world.

Above: *About 8 miles (13km) to the north of Sandwood Bay is Cape Wrath, the most north-westerly point of the British mainland.*

ISLE OF SKYE

*T*he Isle of Skye is the second largest of the Hebridean Islands
after Lewis, with an area of almost 700 square miles (1,126 square km).
In walking terms, it's best known for the Cuillin, a breathtaking range
of dark and angular mountains on the Minginish peninsula, the traverse
of which is widely regarded as among the finest mountain adventures in
the whole of Britain. But the opportunities for coastal walking are also
immensely varied and high quality, thanks in part to the island's
geography, which sees its five main peninsulas radiate out in all
directions. Nowhere on Skye are you more than 5 miles (8km)
from the sea.

Where the Mountains Meet the Sea

The two contrasting routes outlined here give a flavour of Skye's wonderful coastline. The walk out to the low and exposed peninsula of Rubh' an Dùnain from Glen Brittle has plenty of close-up historical interest, with ancient cairns and the ruined crofts of a 19th-century settlement. However, the far-off views will also distract you, including the distant prospect of the Small Isles and the southern Outer Hebrides, and, towering above the peninsula like a colossus, the mighty Cuillin ridge.

The second route provides a totally different spectacle, with a popular woodland track out to the high cliffs of the Duirinish peninsula, where Macleod's Maidens are among the finest sea stacks on Skye. Both walks provide a useful reminder that you don't need to be an expert mountain type to enjoy this wonderful island on foot, a point reinforced by Andrew Dempster's recent account of his 360-mile (579-km) walk around the entire coastline of Skye (see the information panel on page 116). Apart from being a lively and engrossing narrative, it also introduces you to some of the other terrific coastal walks awaiting you on Skye: Rubha Hunish at the tip of Skye's northernmost peninsula of Trotternish, especially rich in seabirds; a tour of the lonely Waternish Point, where you can watch for whales and other passing cetaceans; and the walk out to the lighthouse on Neist Point at the far end of the Duirinish peninsula.

Right: *The mighty peaks of the rugged Cuillin Hills provide a spectacular backdrop to the Rubh' an Dùnain walk.*

Walk 1: Rubh' an Dùnain

The walk starts at the beach car park at Glen Brittle, a popular departure point for small groups of seriously fit and well-equipped hillwalkers heading for the peaks of the Cuillin, which rise spectacularly above the sea loch. There's also a youth hostel, mountain rescue post and, near the beach, a campsite – the latter has handy toilets and a shop selling ice cream and cold drinks; both are open to the public. Despite its popularity with walkers and other holidaymakers, Glen Brittle remains a peaceful and unspoilt location, so it's a little odd to imagine planes coming in to land.

Previous pages: *Evening sunlight on the Cuillin, with the moorland track beside Loch Brittle in the foreground.*

WALK 1: RUBH' AN DÙNAIN

Start/finish: *Glen Brittle (beach car park)*

Distance: *8 miles/13km*

Time: *4 hours/1 day*

Terrain: *Low peninsula of rough vegetation and rocky outcrops, plus quite a few boggy sections, especially after rain.*

Ordnance Survey map: *Explorer 411 Skye: Cuillin Hills.*

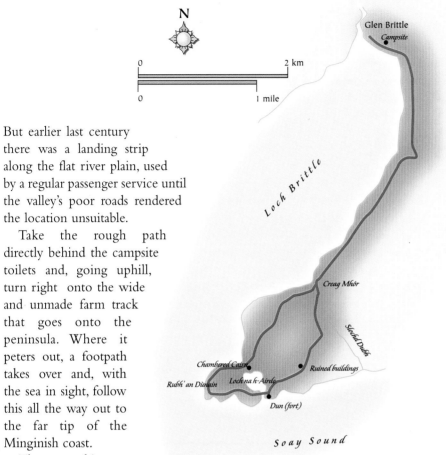

But earlier last century there was a landing strip along the flat river plain, used by a regular passenger service until the valley's poor roads rendered the location unsuitable.

Take the rough path directly behind the campsite toilets and, going uphill, turn right onto the wide and unmade farm track that goes onto the peninsula. Where it peters out, a footpath takes over and, with the sea in sight, follow this all the way out to the far tip of the Minginish coast.

The route skips over one or two pleasant burns that, after a heavy shower in the hills above, can get a little frisky, and passes below the basalt cliffs of Creag Mhór, which attract climbers when the Cuillin is in cloud. Across on the far shore of Loch Brittle, the steep slopes plunge down to the water, and a little further up the coast give rise to towering sea cliffs and the jagged tooth of Stac an Tuill.

Rubh' an Dùnain, which is pronounced 'roo an dunan', may not be especially high, but as you venture further, the views out to sea become more expansive. Given clear weather, the outline of South Uist and Barra on the Outer Hebrides can first be seen away to the south-west; then less than 10 miles (16km) away due south are the Small Isles of Canna and Rum (that's the mountainous one in the middle), with Eigg mostly hiding behind Rum. Finally, as you round the tip, the low island of Soay just a mile or so offshore becomes apparent. If the weather is decent, the hills of the mainland will also be visible, including the lofty outline of the Knoydart peninsula.

Signs of the Past

Once you've soaked up the offshore views, turn your attention to the headland itself, for despite its ostensibly featureless character it has plenty of stories to tell.

Towards the far end is Loch na h-Airde, above which sits a chambered cairn that, when first excavated in 1932, yielded the remains of six people, plus some pottery. The grassed-over roof of the central chamber has since fallen in, but the passageway remains intact. Nearby is a small cave where further items of pottery dating from the Beaker period were discovered, plus some evidence of an Iron Age forge. The loch itself is a small, rather marshy affair that is nowadays the preserve of birds and other wildlife, but at some point in the past its southern outflow was widened into a channel to connect with the sea. It has been suggested that it was created as long ago as the Viking period, to provide them with a safe harbour, but it is probably of more recent construction.

On the eastern side of the channel the modest promontory is topped by a fort (*dun*), after which the headland is named. The Iron Age defence is defined by an impressive, 13-foot-high (4-metre) drystone wall, while cliffs guard its seaward face.

A Place to Linger

From the fort, wander back across the headland – there are a few sheep tracks and minor paths, but beware some patches of bog – and if the summer bracken isn't too high you will see evidence of much more recent habitation on the peninsula. The ruined buildings were once home to the MacAskills, who acted as lookouts or coastguards for the Clan MacLeod; until the 1880s there were as many as 20 crofting families living out here on this remote headland.

Rubh' an Dùnain today is an uninhabited and peaceful spot. It's somewhere to linger and soak up the atmosphere and views, whether you gaze out dreamily at the other islands or keep your eyes peeled for passing dolphins and whales (killer, pilot and minke are all occasionally seen off Skye's northern and western shores). Or, as I did, you may choose to find a peaceful spot in the shelter of a wall and fall fast asleep for an hour. On Rubh' an Dùnain, it really doesn't matter.

The prospects of getting seriously lost on the headland are fairly slim, for a long, firm wall crosses the entire peninsula along the sunken line of Slochd Dubh, a natural fault that translates as

Below: *The Rubh' an Dùnain walk begins at the head of Loch Brittle, a sheltered sea loch.*

the 'black pit'. When you reach this, turn left and follow it back to join the track from Glen Brittle. The return is enlivened by the fantastic spectacle of the Cuillin directly ahead. It's sometimes called the Black Cuillin, since it's made up of a hard, dark igneous rock known as gabbro, which contrasts with the smoother and more rounded granite peaks of the Red Cuillin further east.

You can vary the final half mile or so by dropping down the hillside to a minor path above the shore. For a souvenir of your visit, you could do worse than make the small detour off the lane back at Carbost to visit Skye's famous Talisker distillery, where the highly regarded peaty-flavoured single malt whisky has been produced since 1830 when Hugh and Kenneth MacAskill founded the first still. Now, does that family name ring a few bells?

Above: The snow-topped peaks of the mighty Cuillin Ridge, as seen from Loch Brittle, are a real draw for rock climbers and hillwalkers alike.

Walk 2: Macleod's Maidens

Before you begin your journey out to Idrigill Point, take a moment to look around the small community of Orbost. The Orbost Estate was purchased by the Highland and Islands Enterprise in 1997 to provide, as they put it, sustainable rural development, including new smallholdings and housing, amenity woodland and organic agriculture. As a result, new crofting plots have been established, as well as several unobtrusive commercial units and small-scale agricultural enterprises (the polytunnels are a rare sight on the open, windy shores of Skye).

115

WALK 2: MACLEOD'S MAIDENS

Start/finish: *Orbost (car park)*

Distance: *11½ miles/18.5km*

Time: *6 hours/1 day*

Terrain: *Firm forest tracks, then an undulating and occasionally boggy path out to the rough clifftop.*

Ordnance Survey map: *Explorer 407 Skye: Dunvegan.*

Guidebook: 25 Walks in Skye and Kintail *by Hamish Brown (Mercat Press);* Skye 360: Walking the Coastline of Skye *by Andrew Dempster (Luath Press).*

Public transport and general information: *Portree Tourist Information Centre (01478 612137), www.aros.co.uk (Skye visitor centre).*

Woodland Miles

The route out to Macleod's Maidens is popular and well walked, and begins at the public car park by Orbost Farm. Walk along the vehicle track past Orbost House, and soon this swings down to and around the sheltered inlet of Loch Bharcasaig. Go through a gate past the bayside cottages and out along a wide forest drive parallel with the shore. Although a dense plantation to begin with, you will soon emerge into an area that has been recently felled, allowing expansive views across Loch Bracadale with its fish farms and small islands that contain numerous arches and caves. Further on along the track you can even make out a remarkable double arch on one of the headlands opposite, allowing you to see the water surging through both at once.

Beyond a gate and a ford, the forestry track gives way to a pleasant path that climbs gradually up a wide corridor among the young conifers. Keep your eyes peeled for birds of prey, including buzzards, kestrels, merlins, hen harriers and, of course, the rare sea eagle (see page 119).

Rebel With a Cause

The route out to the end of the headland skirts the shoulder of Beinn na Moine and drops down above Brandarsaig Bay to pass through a gate in a newly erected fence. The high barrier is designed to deter deer, since this rough and undulating hillside has been newly planted with saplings. Part of a project called Future Forests, it's been named Rebel's Wood in honour of the late Joe Strummer, lead singer with the rock group The Clash. It might seem a little odd to associate the strident tones of The Clash with a peaceful corner of Skye, but there again Joe Strummer (who died in 2002) was always one of the more intelligent and interesting of Britain's post-punk exponents. He was also passionate about trees and forests, and concerned about the amount of carbon dioxide emissions generated by the music industry – from the pressing of millions of CDs to the huge travelling entourage of touring bands. So he decided that one way of offsetting the damage was to plant a woodland, and the Future Forests project was born.

To date, over 2,500 of his fans have sponsored individual

Below: *Chambered cairns on low-lying peninsulas such as Rubh' an Dùnain indicate early settlement.*

tree plantings at Rebel's Wood – ranging from rowan and birch through to alder, oak and willow – which have been carried out by local people via the Orbost Trust. A handsome elm bench has also been positioned beside the path for visitors to enjoy the views and admire the emerging woodland. It's a worthy legacy to a fine artist and principled man, and if you want to contribute, go to www.futureforests.com.

Skye Clearances

Although today the peninsula is quiet and the preserve of the foresters, shepherds and, of course, the wildlife, there was at one time a small and isolated community out here, and shortly the route passes through a jumble of grassed-over ruins.

Like so many other tiny coastal settlements on Skye, Idrigill was cleared to make way for the grazing of sheep. With the decline of the traditional clan system following the Jacobite defeat in 1746, agricultural practices began to change and the drovers and their familiar herds of cattle were replaced by vast flocks of sheep. Throughout the next century whole communities were forcibly uprooted to make way for this new and, for the landowner at least, valuable economic commodity, with many leaving en masse to begin a new life in Canada, the United States and Australia. However, a few of Skye's crofters decided to resist, and in April 1882 men, women and children from the Braes, east of Sligachan, fought a pitched battle with over 50 policemen sent from Glasgow to evict them. The Royal Commission that followed looked into their grievances and eventually led to the Crofters' Holding Act of 1886 that enshrined their rights of tenancy in law.

Below: The Duirinish peninsula provides fantastic views across to the Cuillin Hills.

Views of the Shapely Maidens

Beyond Idrigill, follow the path as it veers away from the cliffs to go through a short, narrow valley between the modest heights of Ard Beag and Steineval and finally emerge near Idrigill Point. Go through the gate in the new fence and out onto the headland. A cairn is positioned on the clifftop above the sea stacks known as Macleod's Maidens.

The three rocky pinnacles supposedly represent the wife and two daughters of the fourth chief of Clan Macleod, who were drowned at the location when their boat was driven onto the rocks. The largest of the Maidens (the mother, of course) is 210 feet (65 metres) tall, making it the highest sea stack on Skye. When seen from the sea it apparently has an uncanny resemblance to statues of a seated Queen Victoria. The other two Maidens (the daughters) are joined at their base by a raised ledge, and they appear to be sitting obediently at the foot of their mother. The stacks are just one stunning natural feature on this dramatic if inhospitable coast, which over the years has been responsible for numerous wrecks. According to tales, though, lights were sometimes placed at the foot of the Maidens to deliberately lure boats onto the Black Skerries (An Dubh Sgeir), a notorious group of rocks a little offshore.

To get the best views of the Maidens themselves, walk a little further westwards along the clifftop above Inbhir a Gharraidh and look back to see the three stacks in profile. The open, undulating terrain of heather and rabbit-nibbled turf is generally easy to walk, but the actual cliff-edge is prone to crumbling and requires the utmost caution. These are high and unfenced cliffs with sheer drops, so keep back from the edge and beware sudden gusts of wind and the slippery grass slopes after rain.

Discovering Duirinish

How far along the cliffs you walk depends on the prevailing weather and how much time you have at your disposal – bearing in mind that you have the return leg to come. Certainly, there are some stunning arches, caves and waterfalls the further west you venture, with a stretch of

THE RETURN OF THE SEA EAGLE

The white-tailed sea eagle is, without doubt, Britain's most magnificent native bird of prey. Until it was persecuted to domestic extinction early last century, there were as many as 100 eyries among the remote islands and coastal areas of north-west Scotland. The last of the 'original' breeding sea eagles was shot over Soay Sound in 1916, near one of the walks featured here, but 60 years later chicks from nests in northern Norway were brought to the nearby island of Rum. After ten years of round-

the-clock monitoring and protection a pair successfully fledged a chick, and there are now over 30 pairs throughout Scotland – including Skye. For a proper introduction to the island's most majestic resident make sure to visit the Aros visitor centre near Portree, where knowledgeable RSPB staff will show you live CCTV images (the 'nestcam') of a sea eagle's nest on the island. They'll also tell you what to look out for if you see a large bird circling in the air above, although with a truly awesome wingspan of 8 feet (2.4 metres) and a pronounced head and wedge-shaped tail, the sea eagle (the fourth largest eagle in the world) is fairly hard to mistake. Unlike the golden eagle they are true coastal birds, nesting on cliffs and in trees. If you are lucky enough to see one, make sure to complete a sea eagle sighting record form, available at Aros.

wild and uninhabited cliffs that many consider the finest (as well as the most challenging) coastal walking on the whole of the island. Strong walkers could continue via the bothy in Glen Ollisdal to Glen Dibidal (roughly 3 miles/5km west of the Maidens), then head inland to return to Orbost, possibly via the flat-topped summit of Macleod's Table South (Healabhal Bheag). Alternatively, experienced types may consider developing the coastal walk into a linear outing via the stunning cliff-line of the Hoe. Despite the map indicating otherwise, there is no defined track, rather a series of soaring and precipitous cliff faces topped with rough pasture and moorland, and interspersed by several deep-cut valleys. It's an adventurous outing, and you will also need to arrange collection at Ramasaig, or further on near Neist Point.

For those content with simply reaching the Maidens, which is a more than satisfying walk in its own right, of course, the return is back the same way.

Left: The rugged cliffs west of Macleod's Maidens draw the equally rugged walker on further round the Isle of Skye.

119

ISLE OF ARRAN

As you steam into Brodick on the Caledonian MacBrayne ferry from Ardrossan, it's hard not to be captivated by Arran's superb mountain outline rising invitingly above the bay. No wonder that the island, often described as Scotland in miniature, is so popular with visitors. It's neat and accessible, with everything in perfect proportion ~ from the shapely bays and beaches with a scattering of small coastal communities, to the grand central mountain group fashioned by the glaciers. Apart from the walking options, there are cycle routes and golf courses, boat trips and paragliding; if it rains you can always head under cover with a visit to the Heritage Museum or the island's new brewery near Brodick. But, as elsewhere on Scotland's frequently stunning west coast, there are also miles of largely unspoilt and comparatively unexplored coastline to discover.

Beachcombing Tranquil Shores

Compared to the island's well-known hills, Arran's attractive shoreline has been rather underexposed. But if you want an alternative to the procession of walkers who clog the summit path to Goatfell, why not explore the newly created Arran Coastal Way? About 63 miles (101km) long, the trail mostly hugs the island's shoreline, which varies in nature from pristine sandy bay to wave-cut platform and chaotic boulder field. It takes advantage of the raised beach that almost entirely encircles the island, and which makes for a useful walking corridor when the ground behind gets more severe. Since Arran's main road does likewise, the two routes sometimes have to share the same strip of land, which, although not ideal, does mean that the island's decent bus service makes linear coastal walking a car-free option. However, there are two sections of the coastal way that are entirely away from the road (although buses serve each end), and these form the two walks outlined here. At the north of the island there's a popular coastal path from Lochranza round the Cock of Arran, which although well walked and mostly straightforward does include one short, rock-strewn section. The views across to Bute and Argyll are particularly outstanding, and on a clear day the mountains on the mainland stand out crystal-clear.

At the opposite end of the island, the stretch from Lagg to Whiting Bay follows no established path but instead traces an unblemished shoreline of tiny, sandy beaches and falls of jumbled rocks. There is plenty of hopping from boulder to boulder, especially below the cliffs at Dippen Head and Bennan Head. At the latter, the narrow rocky foreshore is impassable for a couple of hours at high tide, so time your route accordingly (information on tides is available from the tourist information centre). Some of the terrain is quite rough and it will undoubtedly take you longer than you think, although you can always halve the overall length by finishing at Kildonan – but for the beachcomber, naturalist, geologist and coastal connoisseur, this is high quality stuff. Sometimes you simply don't need to follow a path.

Right: *Huge copper stills are part of the traditional distillery process practised in Arran's award-winning whisky distillery and visitor centre in Lochranza. At one point in the 19th century, there were some 50 whisky distilleries on the Isle of Arran, many of them illegal.*

Previous pages: *The clear waters of the Atlantic Ocean lap the shore near the Cock of Arran.*

WALK 1: LOCHRANZA TO SANNOX

Start: *Lochranza*

Finish: *Sannox*

Distance: *10 miles/16km*

Time: *5 hours/1 day*

Terrain: *Low-level coastal track, occasionally boggy at first; one area of rocks requires some care.*

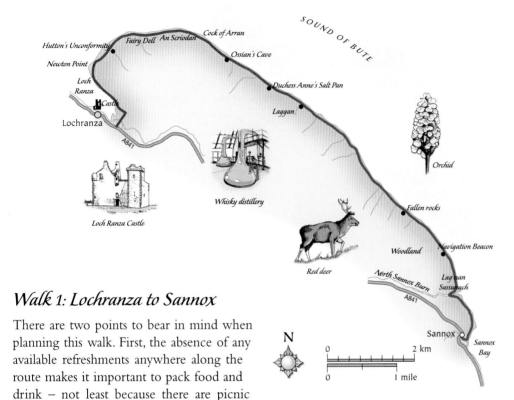

Whisky distillery

Loch Ranza Castle

Orchid

Fallen rocks

Navigation Beacon

Woodland

Red deer

North Sannox Burn

Laggan Sassunach

A841

Sannox

Sannox Bay

Hutton's Unconformity

Fairy Dell

An Scriodan

Cock of Arran

Ossian's Cave

Newton Point

Loch Ranza

Castle

Lochranza

A841

Duchess Anne's Salt Pan

Laggan

SOUND OF BUTE

Walk 1: Lochranza to Sannox

There are two points to bear in mind when planning this walk. First, the absence of any available refreshments anywhere along the route makes it important to pack food and drink – not least because there are picnic spots aplenty. The second factor comes into play if you are walking between mid-August and mid-October, for this part of Arran, including the coastline, is used for deerstalking. As many as 2,000 red deer live on northern Arran; when they are culled each autumn, a section of the coastal route is occasionally closed or diverted. Check in advance with the tourist information centre or call the Hillphone Answering Service, a round-up of local access information that is updated daily (see information panel on page 126).

Sampling a Wee Dram

The walk begins by the secluded, sheltered inlet of Loch Ranza. It's dominated by the remains of a late-16th-century castle, a typical Scottish tower house thought to have been constructed on top of an earlier building and supposedly the inspiration for the castle in Herge's Tintin adventure *The Black Island*. The community of Lochranza has changed a bit since its days as a busy herring port, with many of its visitors now heading for the campsite, youth hostel and field study centre, or for the ferry connection with Claonaig on the Kintyre peninsula. Another local attraction is Arran's only whisky distillery, which when it opened in the mid-1990s became the first on the island for 150 years. It produces the Arran Single Malt, which they say is maturing exceptionally well. If you want to learn more about the art of distilling (and perhaps try the end result), the visitor centre and café is open daily from March to October.

From the main road, follow the lane round to the northern side of the loch and where it ends near Newton Point continue on the well-walked track across the raised beach. This long, grassy strip can be a little boggy in places, but does support a varied plant life, including orchids.

A little further on is a location known as Hutton's Unconformity, which is where the eminent 18th-century geologist Dr James Hutton made a little bit of geological history. Arran is one of Britain's foremost sites for the study of geology, since this relatively small island has an incredibly complex make-up, and it was on a field trip in 1787 that Hutton struck upon his

Theory of the Earth. He was able to identify here, near Lochranza, that rocks of different ages rested at odd angles against each other. This unconformity helped him demonstrate a number of important principles, and ultimately determine the age of the Earth. It might not sound much to a casual bystander, but in the world of geology this is the equivalent of a sacred site.

After a pleasant grassy section by the cottage at Fairy Dell, there's a short but rough sandstone boulder field called An Scriodan before the shoreline track reasserts itself and the walking becomes much easier. Along the way you pass the Cock of Arran, a massive sandstone boulder which, until the head was broken off, was said to have resembled a giant cockerel. Today you have to use your imagination.

You have to do likewise at Duchess Anne's Salt Pan, the name given to a collection of now derelict buildings where salt was extracted from the seawater in the early 1700s. This industry was facilitated by the local discovery of coal, which enabled the seawater to be evaporated in the salt pan. In its day, Arran salt was considered especially pure and highly valued.

A View of Scotland

The rest of the walk is pleasantly straightforward and easy to follow, with the track occupying the narrow coastal shelf between the rocky shore and steeply sloping hills behind. There's an isolated cottage at Laggan, several large caves (mostly back from the shoreline, including Ossian's Cave some way uphill), and ample opportunities for a wander down to the water's edge and a spot of beachcombing, or perhaps a picnic stop and a chance to gaze out across the water to the mainland. Looking clockwise, the edge of Kintyre is across to your left (west), while directly ahead is the mouth of Loch Fyne and the Cowal peninsula. On the far side of the Sound of

Below: *The village of Lochranza looks out to the northern part of the Kintyre peninsula. The 40-mile-long (64-km) peninsula considers itself Scotland's only 'mainland island', being connected to the rest of Scotland by the narrow isthmus of Tarbert, but in all other aspects resembling a western isle such as Arran.*

Bute is Bute itself, although it's difficult to distinguish its outline since the island is so close to the mainland. As the coastline path steadily swings eastwards there are new views towards the Cumbrae Islands (Little and Great), nestling off the shore south of Largs, and the Argyll coast.

Closer to home, you may be puzzled by several large white gantries, complete with lights, erected in a vertical line on the hillside immediately above. These turn out to be artificial beacons used by shipping for speed trials – navigational mileposts, in effect – and of course there are several more at regular intervals along the coast.

The first of the beacons is at a place called Laggantuin. If you look closely you will see the outlines of several buildings, for like nearby North Sannox, this was once a farmstead until its inhabitants were evicted in 1829 to make way for the landlord's sheep flock – another sad chapter in the Highland Clearance. The families sailed to North America and ultimately settled in Megantic County in Lower Canada.

Beyond another fall of giant boulders, this time easily negotiated, you pass through a gate in the deer fence and join a long, easy woodland track through the spruce and hazel to the mouth of North Sannox Burn. Here, by the picnic site and toilets, is an informative Forestry Commission noticeboard explaining that the picnic site – which in the summer often echoes to the sounds of English accents – is close to Lag nan Sassunach (Hollow of the English), where Cromwell's soldiers, killed near Sannox at Clach a' Chath (Stone of the Fight), were supposedly buried.

The official coastal path now follows the lane up to the coast road, then turns left for the short walk into Sannox. If conditions permit, a more attractive option is to cross the shallow river via stepping-stones (or wading if the water is low) for a well-used track above the shore around to the mouth of Sannox Burn. Here you must take a broad, straight path through the gorse behind the sandy beach, which will bring you out by the two small car parks. Across the road begins a wonderful path up Glen Sannox to Cir Mhor and Goatfell – but that's an adventure for another day.

Above: *The northern coastline of Arran contains unusual rock formations and several boulder fields, which make it both physically and geologically distinct from the south of the island.*

Above: A Neolithic burial site marks the start of the walk near Lagg.

Walk 2: Lagg to Whiting Bay

The start of this walk may momentarily confuse, since it begins next to the Kilmory Post Office Stores, which is seemingly in the hamlet of Lagg. Meanwhile, the Torrylinn Creamery (with cheese-making displays) is just up the hill in Kilmory in one direction, while the Lagg Inn (a welcoming old coach house) is a couple of minutes' walk the other, so I presume it's simply one of those things… Despite this, there is a clear sign next to the shop that points along a lovely woodland track to Torrylinn chambered cairn. Situated on the low clifftop, this much-disturbed Neolithic burial site would probably have been the last communal resting place for members of one of the several small agricultural settlements that dotted this fertile shore.

The path continues beyond the cairn to an old farmhouse, after which it drops down to the beach via a farm track. Here it's simply a question of turn left and follow the unspoilt shoreline eastwards. For almost a mile there's a narrow but gloriously untainted strip of sand, but gradually the rocks take over and there are some wonderfully eroded and wave-carved specimens for you to inspect. If the sea is out you can clamber over them quite easily or, better still, take to the low grassy sward behind, where for much of the way there is a faint track. It's a little boggy in places, but you will be rewarded with patches of wild irises. Further on, the sloping, south-facing banks are home to tufts of thrift or sea pink, and also the white flowers of sea campion, sometimes growing in little clumps between boulders.

WALK 2: LAGG TO WHITING BAY

Start: *Lagg*

Finish: *Whiting Bay*

Distance: *10 miles/16km*

Time: *7 hours/1–2 days*

Terrain: *Shoreline route including sandy bays and rough grassy sward, but boulder fields make for hard going in places. The foot of Bennan Head, by Black Cave, is impassable at high tide.*

Ordnance Survey map: *Explorer 361 Isle of Arran.*

Guidebook: *Isle of Arran Coastal Way (map and guide) by Hugh McKerrell.*

Public transport: *Arran Area Transport Guide from information centre, or go to www.spt.co.uk.*

Information: *Brodick Tourist Information Centre (01292 678100); Hillphone Answering Service (deerstalking information; 01770 302363); www.coastalway.co.uk.*

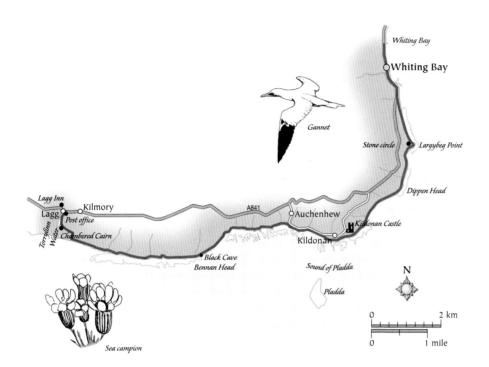

Flotsam and Jetsam

Hugh McKerrell, co-creator of the Arran Coastal Way, points out in his booklet guide that the sea to the south of this point is clear all the way to northern Spain, so the fetch can be quite dramatic. It is certainly a veritable Aladdin's Cave for beachcombers, with all manner of driftwood, fishing tackle, packaging and general rubbish washed up on the strand line. Based on the evidence here, the amount of plastic bottles, in particular, that must be floating around our oceans is quite staggering, and while plastic bags take 10 to 20 years to break down and tin cans around 50 years to biodegrade, plastic bottles remain indefinitely. To work out where some of the flotsam (wreckage) and jetsam (stuff thrown overboard) might come from, take a close look at the fishing crates or boxes that are washed up on this shoreline in surprisingly large numbers, as they usually bear the name of the port of origin. On my particular walk I counted over a dozen destinations around the British Isles (from Grimsby and Whitehaven to Eyemouth and Duncannon) and even one from Quimper in Brittany. Can you beat that?

The Cave on the Headland

Towards Bennan Head the coastal shelf narrows and you are forced onto the rocks at the mouth of Black Cave. This is the largest sea cave on Arran, situated dramatically underneath the imposing headland, and worth a cursory exploration. The fact that a shaft of daylight shines through a hole at the top of the back wall indicates another entrance, but it is dark and slippery and not easily accessible. The cave looks like the kind of place that should abound with legends of sea monsters or smugglers. Indeed, the boulders around its entrance are covered by the sea at high tide, so try to time your journey so that your way ahead is clear, or else wait until the water level is safe.

Below: Black Cave, below Bennan Head, is lapped by the sea at high tide and for a while is impassable by walkers.

Right: The unstable and ivy-clad remains of Kildonan Castle can be found behind the village of Kildonan on Arran's southern shore.

Beyond Bennan Head the foreshore widens again, and the sandy beach is punctuated by a succession of distinctive igneous dykes that run from the land out into the water. Where these dark, jagged lines of rocks cluster they are known rather evocatively as a dyke swarm, and they were formed when molten liquid was forced up vertical cracks between the sedimentary rocks. Since the latter are less resistant to erosion, the igneous dykes remain as prominent surface features.

From Auchenhew to Kildonan you can walk the quiet shore road, and refreshments can be found at either of the two hotels. A mile out to sea is the islet of Pladda, topped by a lighthouse; 12 miles (19km) further on is the unmistakable volcanic plug of Ailsa Craig, home to a huge gannet colony and where a granite quarry apparently produces some of the finest curling stones in the world.

SEAL-SPOTTING OFF ARRAN

The shores of Arran are a great place for seeing seals close-up, and these native mammals are often to be seen bobbing in the water or basking on the rocks. On the Lochranza walk look for them at Newton Point at the mouth of the loch; at the south of the island they are often to be seen west of Bennan Head. Of the two types usually spotted off the British coast, you will invariably see the common (or harbour) seal, which has a mottled grey body and a rounded head and snub nose. When it rests on top of a rock with its head and tail raised, it looks a most ungainly creature. How different, though, when it swims in the water, diving for usually 5–10 minutes at a time in search of fish, squid and crab.

The Atlantic grey seal, by contrast, is larger with a 'Roman' nose and a head that is long and flat. They have variable markings and can appear almost black when wet. Unlike common seals, who tend to favour inshore waters, the grey is more adventurous and is often found on remote beaches. As much as 70 per cent of the world's population is thought to live in British coastal waters, but exact figures are hard to come by. Another characteristic of the grey is that it is especially vocal, emitting a range of barks, moans and hisses. Seals are not generally aggressive towards humans, but like all wildlife you should respect their space and admire them from a suitable distance, particularly when they have newly born pups in the early summer.

A Peaceful Conclusion

Kildonan takes its name from St Donan, a 6th-century monk who sailed to Arran with St Columba and established a cell here. Today's elongated and rather scattered community includes the remains of Kildonan Castle, of which little is known and even less survives. The sand gives way to more rocky ledges and platforms, and back from the raised beach the low cliffs are partly covered in vegetation. They rise up in a small crescendo at Dippen Head, where there is an impressive waterfall and yet another boulder field to negotiate. But after Largybeg Point, a low promontory with a small stone circle, the walking is much easier and more straightforward, with the last stretch to Whiting Bay along the edge of the beachside pasture if you prefer.

There are good views across to Holy Island, which is now owned by a group of Tibetan Buddhists and can be reached by a ferry from Whiting Bay. Since the island contains a cave where St Molas began the tradition of solitary contemplation, it seems quite fitting that the monks have recently opened their Centre for Peace and World Health on the island. Here you can participate in workshops and residential courses in the likes of yoga, meditation and t'ai chi. But, after 10 miles (16km) of invigorating coastal walking, you might settle for a pot of tea and a slice of cake at the Pantry tearoom in Whiting Bay instead.

Above: Igneous dykes, originally formed by molten liquid forced up vertical cracks between sedimentary rocks, form prominent surface features that run into the sea along the coast around Kildonan. This one draws the walker's eye towards the islet of Pladda a mile out to sea.

ANGLESEY

A nglesey, or Ynys Môn, is the largest island in England and Wales, and
a unique place. It may be separated from mainland Wales only by the
narrow Menai Strait, but its low, flat interior is a curiously empty
land of rolling green fields and whitewashed buildings that feels more akin to
Cornwall. For the walker, though, it's the 125 miles (201km) of coastline that sets
the island apart, varying from a low shoreline of dunes and fields in the south to
the undulating cliff terrain, pebble coves and sandy bays along the north and
east coasts. This is a splendidly varied seaboard, full of unexpected delights.

Wales's Best-kept Secret

For all that Anglesey's interior may feel akin to Cornwall, the island is intensely Welsh, with as many as 70 per cent of its population using Welsh as their first language. Visitors from England and elsewhere (at least those who don't rush headlong across the island to the Holyhead ferry without stopping) would do well to pick up a few words of Welsh. At the very least, it will help with map-reading.

Recent efforts have been made to entice more walkers to the island, with an annual walking festival and the development of the Isle of Anglesey Coastal Path (*Llwybr Arfordirol Ynys Môn*). The route is still in its infancy and, although the attractive waymark featuring a hovering tern is a fairly regular sight, there are still sections (especially on the south side of the island) that are little used and overgrown, as well as others that include lengthy inland diversions. However, where the coastal path is at its best, it is already a quality outing, and this is especially true on the northern coast, which forms the basis for this walk.

Right: *A natural arch at Ynys y Fydlyn, near Carmel Head.*

Views of Holy Island

It begins at the hamlet above Church Bay, called Swtan. This unusual word is the old Welsh name for whiting, which was probably brought ashore here long ago by local fishermen, and Porth Swtan is the other name for Church Bay, so named because it is overlooked by the prominent tower of St Rhuddlad's Church. Next to the car park is a restored *bwthyn*, a traditional 18th-century thatched cottage. It was last inhabited in the 1950s, but thanks to painstaking restoration by craftsmen using wheat-straw thatch with a gorse underthatch,

ANGLESEY

Start: Church Bay

Finish: Moelfre

Distance: 29 miles/47km

Time: 14 hours/2–3 days

Terrain: Mainly low, grass-topped cliffs and rocky foreshore, plus sandy bays and a few lanes.

Ordnance Survey maps: Explorer 262 Anglesey West, 263 Anglesey East.

Guidebook: Isle of Anglesey Coastal Path (laminated route cards with maps).

Public transport: Timetables available locally or go to www.ukbus.co.uk/cgi/anglfram.htm.

Information: Holyhead Tourist Information Centre (01407 762622); Isle of Anglesey Coastal Path Project, Rights of Way Unit, Council Offices, Llangefni, Anglesey LL77 7TW (01248 752300); www.angleseycoastalpath.com.

Note: A short section of the route beyond Ynys y Fydlyn is closed to the public each year from 15 September to 31 January, necessitating a diversion inland along a public footpath and lane.

Previous pages:
The white castellated building of Point Lynas lighthouse is a good landmark for walkers.

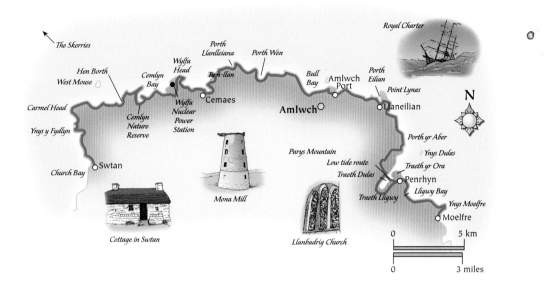

The Skerries

Hen Borth
West Mouse

Carmel Head

Ynys y Fydlyn

Church Bay ○ Swtan

Cottage in Swtan

Wylfa Head
Cemlyn Bay

Wylfa Nuclear Power Station

Cemlyn Nature Reserve

○ Cemaes

Mona Mill

Porth Llanlleiana

Tyn-llan

Porth Wen

Bull Bay

Amlwch ○

Llanbadrig Church

Parys Mountain

Low tide route
Traeth Dulas

Traeth Lligwy

Amlwch Port ○

Porth Eilian

Point Lynas

○ Llaneilian

Royal Charter

N

Porth yr Aber

○ *Ynys Dulas*

Traeth yr Ora

○ Penrhyn

Lligwy Bay

Ynys Moelfre
○ Moelfre

0   5 km

0   3 miles

it's now open again as a folk museum (Friday–Sunday during the summer, plus bank holidays).

Go down past the handily placed Wavecrest Café and follow the sign for the coastal footpath as it takes to the clifftop around the bay, which at low tide reveals a lovely strip of sand. Well walked to start with, the route sticks to the undulating and sometimes pathless, turf-topped cliffs, and although there are few signs, save for some low wooden markers, if you keep fairly close to the sea you shouldn't go wrong. Already it feels quite remote and certainly unspoilt – you won't be surprised to see regular National Trust signs along this coastline – and there should be plenty of wildlife. Look out in particular for choughs, with their distinctive red curved bills, and possibly peregrines and ravens. The cliffs are not especially high compared to Pembrokeshire (perhaps 150 feet/45 metres at their highest), but the layered slate and granite of the Pre-Cambian era makes for ruggedly attractive headlands, riven with deep, dark inlets that bite sharply into the land.

Below: Cemlyn Nature Reserve is one of the most important sites for breeding terns in the whole of Wales.

Away to the far south, the main Anglesey shore mellows and flattens, but instead the eye is drawn to Holy Island, with its distinctive mountain profile. The Isle of Anglesey Coastal Path continues all the way round this small but lofty outpost, and on the far side of Holyhead Mountain in particular there's some great walking to be had with sea stacks and caves. Equally visible is the shipping entering and exiting the port of Holyhead, and a sign at Church Bay warns people using the foreshore and harbour to beware sudden and unexpectedly large waves caused by the huge ferries.

The path drops right down to the water's edge at Ynys y Fydlyn, a beautiful pebbly cove overlooked by two small islands and backed by a shallow lagoon. Beyond this point the coastal trail uses a short, permissive path, which is closed to the public each year from 15 September to 31 January for pheasant shooting.

Aids for Navigation

Offshore is a cluster of small islands and reefs called the Skerries. For centuries they were notorious among seafarers approaching the port of Liverpool. One of their earliest victims was King Charles II's royal yacht, *Mary*, which was wrecked in 1675. Forty years later a lighthouse was established there, and such was its value to passing shipping (who were obliged to pay dues, of course) that eventually it became one of the most lucrative British lighthouses – see the feature below.

Further assistance for nervous mariners is provided by two giant navigational daymarks on the hilltop above you. Popularly known as the White Ladies, they line up with a third beacon on the offshore islet of West Mouse.

By rounding Carmel Head you swing sharply eastwards, and almost immediately the cliffs fall away and the shore becomes quite low and gentle, where fields full of grazing sheep come down virtually to the seashore and wheatears flit from rock to rock. Beyond the pebbly beach at Hen Borth, the field-edge route eventually leads to the nature reserve at Cemlyn, which consists of a brackish lagoon protected from the sea by a curving shingle bank. Although the water is well populated by all manner of wildfowl, the star attractions are the terns, and Cemlyn is one of the most important breeding sites for common, Arctic and sandwich terns in the whole of Wales. As you cross the causeway onto the shingle bank (if the tide is high you may have to walk along the lane instead), there are signs warning visitors to tread carefully, as 'birds nesting on the ridge have well-camouflaged nests, eggs and chicks'. The North Wales Wildlife Trust, who manage the site, have established a line of white posts along the shingle bank; when the terns are nesting between April and July, make sure to walk below and seawards of these markers so as not to disturb the birds.

The high wall by Bryn Aber at the western end was built early last century by Cemlyn's long-time and rather eccentric owner, Captain Vivian Hewitt. A pioneering aviator and racing

TRINITY HOUSE LIGHTHOUSE SERVICE

The lighthouse service of England and Wales is run by Trinity House, constituted under a Royal Charter granted by Henry VIII in 1514, and financed today from light dues, which are levied on vessels calling at ports in the UK. The corporation provides nearly 600 aids to navigation, ranging from lighthouses and radar beacons to light vessels and over 400 buoys. Since 1998 (when North Foreland in Kent was 'de-manned'), all its 72 lighthouses have been automatic, and are controlled from an operations centre at Harwich, Essex. It's a far cry from Europe's first offshore lighthouse, built in wood on the dangerous Eddystone Rock 13 miles (21km) south-west of Plymouth in 1698. It lasted just five years before a storm washed it and its owner away.

The first light on the Skerries, off Anglesey, appeared in 1717, but such was its strategic value to shipping that when it was finally sold to Trinity House in 1841 (the last privately owned lighthouse in British coastal waters), it cost them over £444,000.

The Northern Lighthouse Board administers the 198 lighthouses for Scotland and the Isle of Man. Their last manned lighthouse, Fair Isle, off Shetland, also became automated in 1998. If you want to know more about British lighthouses go to www.trinityhouse.co.uk, or if you are heading for the Cornish walk (pages 10–19), visit the National Lighthouse Museum in Penzance (open daily, Easter–end October).

driver, he was also a passionate ornithologist, and managed the lagoon as a private wildfowl refuge for over 40 years. The wall, which he originally intended to be much higher, was built to create a sheltered area for birds.

Man-made Features

The coastal route returns to the low, grassy shore after its shingle interlude, and soon Wylfa Nuclear Power Station heaves into view. It has to be admitted that this next section is unlikely to figure very highly in most people's top coastal moments, and if that is the case then leapfrog a few miles to Cemaes if you can. Still, power stations are an inescapable feature of the modern British coast – Sizewell, for instance, is plum in the middle of the Suffolk Coast Path (see pages 50–59) – and despite their overbearing size and rigid artificial lines, they exert a certain curiosity value. The coastal path follows a permissive route though the partly wooded and landscaped grounds of the power station (follow the waymarked nature trail), with the added advantage that it passes the entrance of the visitor centre and café (open daily). East of Wylfa Head – *wylfa* means 'lookout' – it's an easy stroll across the fields to reach the houses of Cemaes.

For the benefit of non-Welsh speaking walkers, the name of this large village is pronounced 'Kemm-ice'. It boasts a neat main street that includes a

Above: Wylfa Nuclear Power Station can be seen from some distance along this open coastline. Clumps of sea kale grow among the shingle.

heritage centre/tearoom and the most northerly pub in Wales (The Stag). When seen from afar, the little place seems overshadowed by the clusters of wind turbines that dominate the surrounding hilltops, but in some ways the recent proliferation of wind power units is simply a modern echo of the time when old-fashioned windmills were a common sight across Anglesey. The plentiful supply of corn led to a thriving milling industry, powered by both wind and water, and records from 1929 show that there were 37 windmills operational across the island. Today, you can still see the towers of the windmills, minus their sails, which have been converted into private dwellings.

The Legacy of St Patrick

From the far side of Cemaes's crescent-shaped beach (Traeth Mawr), the coast path climbs back up through the fields to reach Llanbadrig Church at Ty'n-llan. One of the very few Welsh churches named after St Patrick, legend has it that the fifth-century missionary was shipwrecked on Ynys Badrig (St Patrick's Island, also called Middle Mouse) just offshore from here, but managed to make it across and lived for a while in a cave below the site of the church. Considerably altered over the centuries, the building's restoration in the mid-1800s was particularly noteworthy, since its chief benefactor Lord Stanley of Alderley insisted that the building contain elements of his Muslim faith. This can be seen in the blue glass of the East Window, in particular, and with the blue tiles around the Sanctuary.

The location of the church, in a small hollow high up on the cliff-edge, is stunning, and this sets the scene for the next few miles to Amlwch. The cliffs are much steeper now and the path climbs and drops sharply among the bracken and gorse. It's a rugged landscape and, with clumps of heather and rocky outcrops, it has a touch of moorland about it. Above all, though, this is another unspoilt and out-of-the-way stretch, with no car parks or caravan lots to spoil the view. And the few buildings you do come across are mostly redundant remains, such as the derelict china-clay works at Porth Llanlleiana. The same is true a little further on at Porth Wen, where the western side of the wide bay contains the chimneys and well-preserved circular kilns of the old brickworks.

Tea in the Sail Loft

The waymarks continue to guide you eastwards, although for the most part the route is quite obvious. After the houses and hotels of Bull Bay, there's another short burst of cliff path before, swiftly dodging the chemical plant and housing estate at Amlwch, you drop down to the narrow quayside of Amlwch Port, tucked away in a deep creek. There's plenty of interest here, not least because the well-preserved 18th-century port once exported vast amounts of local copper ore from nearby Parys Mountain (at one point the world's most productive copper mine), and later housed several busy shipyards. It also boasted Anglesey's largest windmill, called Mona Mill, which was built in 1816 and at 60 feet (18 metres) high contained seven floors and soon became a landmark for passing ships. Unfortunately it was struck by lightning in 1876, killing the miller's son, and it went out of use soon after. For more on the history of the port, as well as the local

mining industry, make sure to visit the Heritage Centre in the former sail loft above the harbour. It has an unusual sloping floor, with the first floor supported by ships' masts and the window lintels made from ships' timbers. The centre also contains a café, and is open daily in season.

Beyond the sheltered pebbles of Porth Eilian, the trail next crosses the neck of Point Lynas. By the lighthouse on the headland is an old semaphore station, one of a chain along the north Wales coast between Holyhead Mountain and Liverpool that were built in the 1820s to give Liverpool merchants advance notice of their incoming ships. Others were sited on Puffin Island and Great Ormes Head. Messages could be relayed from Anglesey to Liverpool in as little as four minutes. There was also a pilot station

Above: *A calm sea at Moelfre, but 150 years ago this was the scene of a great maritime disaster when the Royal Charter clipper sunk, taking 450 souls down with it.*

here, founded in 1766 as a base for experienced pilots who would guide vessels into the port.

Now your direction shifts southwards, and if the wind has been blowing you may begin to feel the benefit of Anglesey's sheltered eastern side. Sheep and cattle munch contentedly in the open fields of pasture that slope down to the cliff edge. And this, for the most part, is where the trail remains, but above Porth yr Aber the route is forced inland. Via successive fields and a long, partly wooded lane, it turns left to descend to the vast shallow estuary of Traeth Dulas (*traeth* meaning 'beach').

The official route now skirts the northern edge of Traeth Dulas until it reaches the A5025, then returns to the coast via a hilltop path that begins behind the Pilot Boat pub. However, a low-tide option (saving 2 miles/3km) is simply to walk straight across the sand and resume the lane opposite. When the sea is out it is virtually all sand and firm mud, and I found that if you choose your spot carefully the solitary channel is little more than ankle deep – but you *must* be sure of the state of the tide first, since the tidal race can be powerful. Off Dulas Bay you will notice a small island (Ynys Dulas) with a strange-looking tower. This tower was built in the 19th century as a navigational aid and a refuge for stranded sailors, and emergency supplies were stored in it.

The Sinking of the Royal Charter

After the rugged cliffs and exposed headlands of the earlier part of the walk, the route finishes with much gentler and more user-friendly scenery. As a result, the coast is more populated and the caravan parks and sunbathers more numerous. Perhaps the best location is enjoyed by the campers at Penrhyn, as the coast path encircles the well-positioned site that lies between the two unblemished sandy bays of Traeth yr Ora and Traeth Lligwy. Lligwy Bay, in particular, offers a wide and accessible strip of golden sand that in the height of summer is likely to be packed with holidaymakers. No wonder the two car parks are so large, although the upper of the two sports a useful seasonal kiosk and toilets.

As the houses of Moelfre begin to peep over the low headland, you pass a memorial to the victims of a maritime disaster that happened near here almost 150 years ago. It was October 1859, and the *Royal Charter*, a three-masted, steam-assisted clipper, was on the final leg of her journey from Melbourne in Australia to Liverpool, and looking forward to completing the long voyage in a record time of less than 60 days. However, as the ship passed Holyhead in the late afternoon, an almighty storm was blowing up, and as the evening wore on it quickly developed into a terrifying Force 12 hurricane. The *Royal Charter* was driven on to the rocks north of Moelfre in the early hours (one of 133 ships sunk around the British coast that night); over 450 passengers perished, and £300,000 of gold bullion was also lost. Among the early reporters and witnesses on the scene was novelist Charles Dickens, who spent the Christmas of 1859 here and mentions it in his work 'The Uncommercial Traveller'.

That fearsome night seems a far cry on a peaceful summer's day when, standing on the headland at Moelfre, the sun reflects off a dazzling blue sea and all seems calm and tranquil. Immediately offshore is the tiny islet of Ynys Moelfre and, in the distance, Puffin Island, off the eastern tip of Anglesey at Penmon. Far beyond lies the bulk of Great Ormes Head, appearing to rise from the sea off the Welsh mainland at Llandudno.

Compared to some of the more brash holiday resorts in this part of the world, Moelfre really is a very pleasant location at which to finish the walk. Beyond the lifeboat station is the Seawatch Centre (open Tuesday–Sunday, Easter–end September), with various nautical displays, including relics salvaged from the *Royal Charter*. Below this is the tiny but picturesque harbour and beach, perfectly in proportion to the village and coastline; just up the hill is Ann's Pantry, a licensed café and restaurant where you can reward yourself with a homemade treat at one of the garden tables overlooking the sea.

If you want to continue further, the coastal path carries on to Benllech (2½ miles/4km) and the vast sandy expanse of Red Wharf Bay.

Above: The eastern shores of Anglesey are softer and more sheltered than those on the western side of the island, as seen here at Red Wharf Bay, near Benllech.

PEMBROKESHIRE

Pembrokeshire is unique among Britain's national parks in being predominantly coastal ~ nowhere in it are you more than 10 miles (16km) from the sea. It also boasts the only marine nature reserve in Wales and, for its size, has one of the highest densities of protected environmental sites in Europe. It is a coast that combines rugged cliffs and sandy bays, prehistoric remains and medieval castles, and despite a scattering of towns and industry (old and new), enjoys plenty of natural history ~ from the wonderful array of wild flowers to the grey seals and seabirds. It's no coincidence that this national park has a razorbill for its symbol, although for a real close-up look at the likes of puffins, shearwaters and kittiwakes, it's best to put a day or two aside for a boat trip to one of the offshore islands where the birds congregate.

Puffins and Peregrines

Pembrokeshire's far south-westerly position ensures a generally mild climate, although it can be windy on the clifftops – you'll notice the absence of trees along the walk. The Pembrokeshire Coast Path National Trail, which opened in 1970, stretches 186 miles (299km) from Amroth near Tenby in the south, all the way round the peninsula to St Dogmaels on the coast near Cardigan. Serving much of the coast path (and all of it in this featured section) is a dedicated bus service that runs daily in summer and three times a week in the winter. There are four separate bus routes – the Poppit Rocket, Strumble Shuttle, Celtic Coaster and Puffin Shuttle – which in addition to other scheduled services connect with virtually every road point on the coast path and offer the perfect car-free way to walk the trail.

A Walk Around St Brides Bay

Your journey begins at the southern end of St Brides Bay, a huge sweep of sand and low cliff that in shape is like a giant bite taken out of the Pembrokeshire peninsula. Broad Haven makes

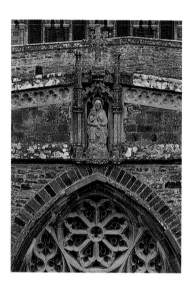

Right: St David's Cathedral in the far west of the county remains a popular destination for tourists and pilgrims alike.

a useful starting point, with cafés and shops, plus a purpose-built youth hostel. From the seafront the well-waymarked coast path goes along the cliffs northwards. The route is obvious enough and, apart from an inland detour approaching Druidston Haven, sticks close to the shore. The reason for the diversion is the cliffside hotel, in the garden of which is a curious building called the Roundhouse. It was built in 1910 as a croquet pavilion by the then owner, Harold Fowler, an international champion of the sport. After this, you drop down to the back of the beach at Druidston Haven, where the freshwater stream makes for a particularly lush valley scene, with tall yellow irises in bloom between May and July.

The clifftop route resumes to Nolton Haven, where you descend past the Mariners Inn to the tiny, picturesque cove squeezed in between the cliffs. Beyond is Rickets Head, an

PEMBROKESHIRE

Start: *Broad Haven*

Finish: *Porthgain*

Distance: *33 miles/53km*

Time: *16 hours/3 days*

Terrain: *Rugged and sometimes challenging cliff scenery, although the high-level path is generally quite firm and interspersed with pleasant sandy bays.*

Ordnance Survey maps: *Outdoor Leisure 35 North Pembrokeshire, 36 South Pembrokeshire.*

Guidebook: The Pembrokeshire Coast Path National Trail Guide *by Brian John (Aurum Press).*

Public transport: *For details of the excellent coastal bus that serves the entire route contact the information centre (below) or go to www.pembrokeshiregreenways.co.uk.*

Information: *St David's Tourist Information Centre (01437 720392); www.pembrokeshirecoast.org.uk.*

Previous pages:
The rugged cliffs of Pembrokeshire's northern coast near Porthgain.

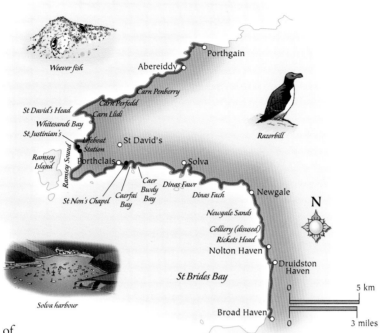

Weever fish

Razorbill

Solva harbour

eye-catching stump of rock jutting out from the cliffs, which signals the start of the glorious, 2-mile-long (3-km) Newgale Sands. Although the path runs along the cliffs at the back, most people don't waste the opportunity to clamber down to the beach and finish the stage by the water's edge. One place to do this is by the disused Trefrane Cliff colliery

Below: *Limekiln by the picturesque and much-used Solva harbour.*

at the southern end of the sands, where the single brick chimney and overgrown spoil heap are all that remains of a small coal-mining industry that once existed at several locations along this coast. The anthracite that was dug here since as far back as the 14th century was said to be of the highest quality, so much so that Queen Victoria specified it for use on her royal yachts.

The beach at Newgale is backed by a high shingle bank, but it has taken some battering over the years. In 1896, the original Duke of Edinburgh pub was destroyed by severe gales, and in 1990 a combination of a fierce storm and high tide swept pebbles across the coast road, blocking it for a week and destroying a telephone box and toilet block in the process. There are also signs warning those going barefoot of the dangers of weever fish. These nasty creatures lie hidden below the surface of the sand at low tide, and standing on their spikes can be particularly painful. Fortunately, the pain is fairly short-lived and can be alleviated by standing in hot water for 20 minutes.

Solva's Hidden Harbour

Beyond Newgale the path clambers back up to the clifftop where it stays all the way to Solva via the National Trust's St Elvis estate and the rugged outcrops of Dinas Fach and Dinas Fawr. By now you will be swinging westwards, and after one or two stiff ascents there is a welcome diversion inland around Solva's picturesque

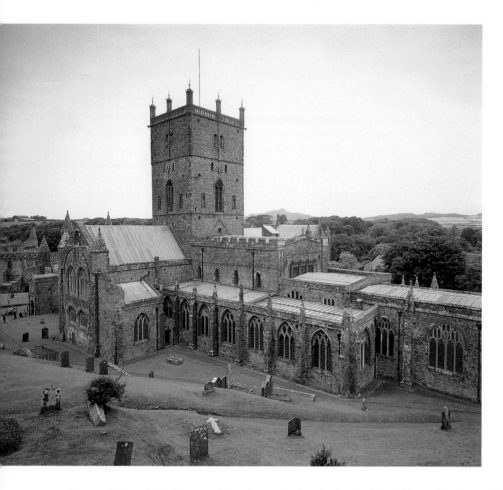

Above: *The cathedral at St David's was built in a hollow of land to protect it from potential enemies.*

inlet. As sheltered harbours go, this surely has to be one of the best, a narrow and crooked finger of water sandwiched between cliffs that reaches deep into the land. If the wind has been blowing or the sun is beating down, you will also be glad for the respite of Solva's wooded shore after 5 miles (8km) of exposed clifftop. The main part of the village is up on the hill, but down by the harbour there are a couple of cafés and pubs, and refreshments are even served at Solva Boat Club on the quayside. Here you will also find some relics from the Smalls lighthouse, the first version of which was built in 1775 to warn shipping of the treacherous Smalls rocks 16 miles (26km) west of the island of Skomer.

The route leaves the quayside and after climbing back onto the cliffs continues in a purposeful fashion along a series of headlands and sheltered coves, boasting fine views back across St Brides Bay and, closer to hand, of a series of caves and natural rock arches that will have your camera clicking. Note in particular the intriguing folds and twists in the strata of the purple sandstone, the same rock that was quarried to build St David's Cathedral.

There are one or two testing climbs, such as around Caer Bwdy Bay, but taken slowly they present no real difficulties, and for long stretches the high path enjoys a firm and level position and is a joy to walk.

Britain's Smallest City

After the caravans at Caerfai Bay you come to St Non's Chapel, supposedly the birthplace of St David during a great storm in AD 462 (St Non being St David's mother). Near the chapel a signpost indicates that you are just a short walk (less than a mile) from St David's itself. (The efficient coast bus service picks up from Porthclais a little further on.) Not much bigger than a large village, thanks to its cathedral St David's is officially Britain's smallest city, given the Queen's formal seal as recently as 1995. A destination for pilgrims and missionaries throughout the Middle Ages, at one stage the Pope announced that two pilgrimages to St David's equalled one to Rome. The famous cathedral was begun in the 1180s, and was built in a dip to hide it from raiders from the sea, while the casket containing the remains of Wales's patron saint is kept behind the high altar.

The next chance for refreshment is at Porthclais, where a seasonal kiosk can usually be found in the National Trust car park. As at Solva, this is another drowned river valley or ria, and over the centuries has been an important port for the movement of trade and goods for St David's and other Pembrokeshire communities. And, like Solva too, the quayside is lined with several well-preserved limekilns, where limestone was brought in by boat and burnt to produce lime that helped enrich the poorer soil. Porthclais also marked the embarkation point for pilgrims on the last stage of the journey to the shrine of St David. It was where the baby David was supposedly baptised by Bishop Elvis, who had sailed over from Ireland specially for the occasion.

Although the chimneys and tankers of Milford Haven oil refinery are visible away to the south, the Broad Haven to Porthgain stretch that you will be walking is entirely unblemished, offering an almost continuous diet of cliffs and breathtaking bays, and nowhere is this more evident than as you approach Ramsey Sound on the far western tip of the mainland. Offshore you will have noticed the scattering of islets and reefs – a danger to shipping but such a spectacle to walkers as the waves crash over them. Across on the southern side of St Brides Bay, the larger islands of Skomer, Skokholm and Grassholm will have been visible for some time, but now you get a close-up view of Ramsey Island as the path swings northwards round to St Justinian's. Ramsey is owned and managed by the Royal Society for the Protection of Birds as a nature reserve and is a key site for nesting seabirds and seals. Although numbers of visitors are carefully controlled, there are daily boat trips and guided walks on the island throughout the summer.

A Hazardous Shore

The lifeboat station at St Justinian's (or, more correctly, Porthstinian) perches high above the water and over the years it has seen plenty of service. Ramsey Island in particular is surrounded by marine hazards of all kinds, including an infamous group of rocks called Bishops and Clerks and another known as the Bitches, plus a formidable tidal race that sweeps through Ramsey Sound at quite a speed. The list of wrecks and loss of life off this coast is considerable, and in 1910 they included three lifeboatmen from St David's who had gone to the aid of a stricken ketch. Mind you, sinking ships usually meant welcome spoil for some people, and crowds of wreckers would gather on the Pembrokeshire cliffs when a vessel was spotted in trouble and heading for the rocks. Sometimes, however, it backfired on them… When a ship returning

Below: *Ramsey Island, seen here from Whitesands Bay, is surrounded by a number of notorious reefs and islets that present a danger to shipping.*

from the West Indies laden with gunpowder was wrecked at Druidston Beach in 1791, there was a free-for-all as people struggled to grab the valuable cargo. Some powder was spilt as barrels were being thrown from the wreck to people waiting below, and when a musket was dashed against a rock, the spark caused the gunpowder to explode. Eight people were killed, and around 60 burnt. The local rector later spoke of the fire as 'providential judgement'.

The Wild Headland

If you only pick up a few words of Welsh, then *llwybr arfordir* will almost certainly be the most useful to you as a walker – it means 'coast path', of course. Following these signs, continue around to Whitesands Bay, or Porth Mawr. This is another stunning little bay, with more surfers being dumped in the foam, more sunbathers lolling about on the beach and another chance for a pot of tea or ice cream. A new visitor centre and café has recently opened by the car park.

You are now embarking on the most remote section of the coast path, much of it well away from human habitation. Around St David's Head in particular the terrain is quite wild and fairly challenging in adverse conditions. The last 10 miles (16km) to Porthgain are scenic and exciting, but remember to pack your sandwiches otherwise your stomach will be rumbling.

St David's Head itself is a relatively modest rocky protuberance, given extra prominence by its sheer wildness. Gone for the moment are the cultivated fields, instead it's a rough and undulating landscape of heather and gorse, grazed by ponies, with plenty of surface rock. Various tracks criss-cross the headland, and a walk out to the point is recommended both for the views and the chance to inspect an ancient stone fortification known as Warrior's Dyke. It dates from the Iron Age and was built to enclose a settlement – the outline of several hut circles can still

Below: Whitesands Bay near St David's Head, is extremely popular with surfers and sunbathers alike.

Left: The raised lifeboat station at St Justinian's was built in 1911–12.

be identified. Now turn tail and follow the route along the clifftop seawards of the impressive angular slopes of Carn Llidi, Carn Perfedd and Carn Penberry (*carn* meaning 'cairn'). The cliffs on this northern shore seem higher and wilder than before, and you're more likely to see peregrine falcons and choughs, and seabirds such as guillemots, razorbills and fulmars, with

THE WILD FLOWERS OF COASTAL PEMBROKESHIRE

One of the most attractive aspects of walking the coast paths of Great Britain is the profusion of wild flowers that burst into life each spring. Different habitats support different plants, of course, but even in seemingly inhospitable environments such as shingle banks and saltmarshes there is often an array of plants that have adapted to suit the conditions.

On the Pembrokeshire cliffs between May and July you will be treated to stunning banks of thrift, or sea pink, interspersed with white sea campion and the delicate yellow flowers of primrose and cowslips. Although primarily a woodland plant, bluebells are still a common sight along the path, as is spring squill, a small bluish-purple flower that dots the grassy clifftops.

A different habitat is provided by the dunes and shingle, where the likes of sea holly and marram grass prevail, while what's known as the splash zone at the foot of the cliffs supports lichens, sea aster and the distinctive yellow-orange heads of golden samphire. Elsewhere, the heaths and grasslands bordering the coastal route are home to orchids and heather, bird's foot trefoil and kidney vetch.

For an accessible general introduction to identifying 48 of the more common wild flowers you will find along the coast path, look out for the national park's leaflet 'Wild Flowers of the Pembrokeshire Coast', available in local tourist information centres.

cormorants and gannets flying out across the waves far below. You will almost certainly spot grey seals as well, which from late summer haul themselves onto the rocks in the coves far below in order to feed their pups. More likely they will be in the sea, a dark blob of a head peering up at you in interest and perhaps puzzlement – just as you stand there and watch them.

Now you're heading north-eastwards, and if it has been blowing you will notice the change of direction. If it's been especially sunny then you may now have the chance to tan the other side of your face, arms and legs.

A Lost Industry

The first real sign of civilization is at Abereiddy, although it doesn't extend much further than a car park and loos. There's the odd house or two, but little to show that as recently as 1938 a slate-quarrying industry supported a community of 50 people here. The quarry was flooded by a severe storm in 1904 and it never reopened; a subsequent typhoid epidemic finished off the small community. As you leave on the path over the headland northwards, you pass the site of the quarry, known as the blue lagoon (it will be obvious why), also what seems to be a small

tower or folly perched on the edge of the cliffs. The origin of this curious little building has been lost to time, but it has been suggested that perhaps it served as a guide for incoming boats, or even that it was used by the quarry directors' wives for their tea parties.

The final clifftop mile or so to Porthgain allows more views along the north coast to Strumble Head, with its prominent lighthouse. Beyond Porthgain the Pembrokeshire Coast Path continues for another 50 miles (80km) via Fishguard to finish at St Dogmaels, on the Afon Teifi near Cardigan. There are more fine cliffs and headlands, but for now your route concludes at Porthgain, a fascinating little port that also contains the remains of the local quarrying industry. A tramway once linked it to Abereiddy for the export of local slate, but granite was also quarried here and clay extracted for bricks. In its day it must have been a hive of activity. The derelict brickworks and empty hoppers make it feel almost like an outdoors museum, a real-life study in industrial archaeology; but fortunately it has a modern, vibrant local community that includes a café/bistro in the converted fishermen's sheds, several galleries and the single-storey 18th-century Sloop Inn. Also check out the harbour for one of Porthgain's best-loved residents – Mervyn the Seal.

Above: Quarrying and brick-making ceased at Porthgain in the 1930s, but its industrial past is still evident.

149

THE GOWER

*T*he Gower is a small and attractive limestone peninsula that sticks out like an oversized big toe from Swansea into the sea off south Wales. Modest in size, its enduring popularity is testimony to its mild climate, sunny disposition and miles of golden sand. They say its 34 miles (55km) of coastline boasts a staggering 70 named beaches, coves and bays. In 1956, the Gower was designated the first Area of Outstanding Natural Beauty in England and Wales – the next step down from a national park – in recognition of its natural diversity and largely unspoilt habitats.

Golden Miles

The Gower's wide-ranging appeal is due in part to its sheer natural diversity, from the limestone cliffs along the southern shore to the saltmarsh and extensive dune systems (known as burrows) mainly found on the western and northern edges. The coast is fringed by considerable tracts of heath and common land, and at the back of several bays there are wildlife-rich deciduous woodlands. The peninsula contains three National Nature Reserves, while smaller reserves, such as Sedgers Bank near Port-Eynon, are managed by Glamorgan Wildlife Trust. The National Trust owns around three-quarters of the coastline, including Rhossili Bay and Worms Head. Inland, the scenery doesn't appear to have changed that much in 100 years, despite the odd caravan. The patchwork of fields is criss-crossed by stone-faced banks and hedges, and around Rhossili the medieval open-field strips known as the Viel (between the church and the headland) still survive to this day.

There is no set coastal trail, as such, and the only local route (the 35-mile/56-km Gower Way) cuts through the middle of the peninsula. Instead, you follow local paths and tracks, sometimes surfaced and well walked via popular bays and beaches, but at other times virtually deserted along high, grassy clifftops and through quiet and intimate woodland. There are plenty of opportunities to paddle – I splashed my way contentedly along virtually the whole length of Rhossili Bay, for instance – and you will rarely be far from a café or pub.

Right: The gatehouse of Oxwich Castle, a fortified Tudor manor house.

The Mumbles Mile

For a walk that is typified by a lack of gaudy seaside development and settlements no bigger than villages, the starting point at the Mumbles may come as something of a surprise, especially if half of Swansea is out promenading. The city bus drops you at the shops overlooking the southern end of the bay, where, among other things, there is a tourist information centre and the remains of the

Previous pages: At Mumbles Head you will turn your back on the city of Swansea and start the walk in earnest.

THE GOWER

Start: The Mumbles

Finish: Llangennith

Distance: 28 miles/45km

Time: 13 hours/2 days

Terrain: From promenade and surfaced paths to rough cliff tracks and sandy bays.

Ordnance Survey map: Explorer 164 The Gower.

Guidebook: Walking Around Gower by West Glamorgan Ramblers' Association.

Public transport: Most buses to the Gower leave from Swansea, where there is a travel shop at the Quadrant Bus Station with full timetables, or go to www.firstgroup.com.

Information: Swansea Tourist Information Centre (01792 468321), the Mumbles (01792 361302).

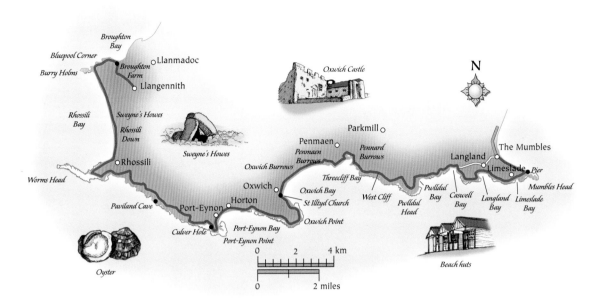

Norman Oystermouth Castle, which like the nearby settlement of the same name comes from the once-busy local oyster-fishing industry.

The Mumbles are closely associated with Swansea's Dylan Thomas who, in his own words, 'was born in a large Welsh town, by a long and splendidly curving shore'. Its unusual name may come from the appearance of the two pale limestone islands off the headland, which are said to look like breasts – in French 'mamelles' or Latin 'mammae'. There are a number of informative noticeboards along the seafront that give more background to the area and its history, including the Mumbles Railway. Built between 1804 and 1806, this ran from Swansea round the bay to the Mumbles and was designed as a freight line, carrying horse-drawn wagons of limestone and coal from the mines in the nearby Clyne Valley. In 1807, an entrepreneur persuaded the owners to allow him to run a passenger carriage along the lines for wealthy visitors and, although this service was short-lived, it is claimed that the line was the first passenger railway in the world.

The first few miles of the walk are along surfaced tracks and are really very easy – just the kind of gentle beginning you need. The pavement of the coast road extends from above the pier at Mumbles Head and snakes round to Limeslade Bay; from here, take to the well-used tarmac path above the low, rocky shore all the way to Langland Bay. Terraced rows of green and white beach huts adorn the seafront, and behind are new apartments and flats, while further up is a mock-Gothic building built as a holiday villa and latterly a convalescent home (almost the same thing, perhaps?). The part-sandy

Left: *Oxwich Burrows are part of a National Nature Reserve, and hundreds of flowering plants can be found among the dunes, marsh and foreshore.*

Right: *The walk to peaceful Fall Bay may not be particularly easy, but the views and solitude it provides on reaching it are well worth the effort.*

sheltered bay is popular with families, but your route continues on round the next headland to reach Caswell Bay, a place beloved by surfers and backed by Bishop's Wood Nature Reserve.

By Pill and Burrow

A short stretch of road-walking is now necessary to bypass a particularly ghastly block of flats. The path should, by rights, pass seawards of them and continue up steps into the wooded cliffs on the far side, but an unstable walkway has rendered the path inaccessible, and at the time of writing you have to walk up the road past Redcliffe Apartments before branching off left on a public footpath back down to the partly wooded cliffs. Here you have a choice of paths – up past a hole in a field that marks the site of a former lead/silver mine, or a lower route along the open, bracken-covered cliffside.

After the beach huts and the bathers of the last few miles, you can now relax and enjoy this much quieter and unspoilt section. Both paths descend to the National Trust's Pwlldu Bay, with its high stony bank and footbridge across the river. All is now serene, but once the Bishopston Valley contained a number of active quarries, from where boats known as limestone tars carried the huge blocks of stone across the Bristol Channel to ports in Devon.

The prominent shingle ridge at the back of the beach is, in fact, the wasted, unwanted detritus of this limestone industry.

On the far side of the bay the path climbs steeply up a sunken track and at the top continues through scrub and fields to emerge at Pwlldu Head. The nearby trig point may only measure 318 feet (97 metres), but it's one of those places that feels higher.

Ahead is Pennard Burrows, a wide and open clifftop corridor where you weave your way between the rocky outcrops and gorse along grassy corridors closely nibbled by rabbits. At Threecliff Bay go over to the stepping stones in order to cross the river. If the Pennard Pill is high ('pill' is the local name for a stream or small river) and the stones are impassable, you must detour upstream to the bridge at Parkmill.

You won't be surprised to learn that Threecliff Bay takes its name from three pointed cliffs at the mouth of the bay. It's a wonderful, gaping sandy spectacle, although signs warn of the dangerous currents where the fresh water issues out into the sea, and swimming is not recommended. At low tide it's possible to walk round to Oxwich Bay, but the more interesting walk is across the low headland of Penmaen Burrows, which includes so-called pillow mounds or artificial burrows that were dug in the Middle Ages to keep rabbits – at the time an important source of meat and fur.

Extracting Salt from Sea Water

Threecliff Bay might have been impressive, but an even broader expanse of sand now reveals itself. Oxwich Bay is almost 2 miles (3km) wide and at low tide the walk across the pristine sand is delightful.

There's no need to enter Oxwich itself, the highlight of which is probably the fortified Tudor manor house of Oxwich Castle. Instead, head back out to Oxwich Point via the diminutive Church of St Illtyd, half hidden in the trees. Beyond this, the path climbs a series of steep steps through a peaceful blanket of oak and ash, then drops down to round the open headland and asume a wave-cut platform at the foot of the cliffs.

Below: *The magnificent broad sandy sweep of Rhossili Bay can be followed at low tide on this walk.*

Port-Eynon Bay is another picturesque sweep of sand, on the far side of which the former lifeboat station has been turned into a youth hostel. The two buoys in the bay mark the spot where the pleasure steamer *Prince Ivanhoe* ran aground in 1981 and was abandoned. Another relic of the past is the old salthouse towards the mouth of the bay. Here, from the 1500s, salt was extracted from a reservoir of seawater and heated in iron pans; the resulting barrel-loads of crystals were shipped out by boat. It was an ideal location for the industry, since the Gower has lower than average rainfall and with very few freshwater rivers feeding into the sea the resulting salinity levels are very high.

On the far side of the low but panoramic headland above Port-Eynon Point is yet another item of interest, but this one will almost certainly leave you puzzled. Culver Hole is a deep chasm in the cliffs which many years ago was enclosed by a massive, 60-foot (18-metre) stone wall – but no one seems to know quite why. The wall contains openings for windows or possibly doors, and suggested uses include a pigeon loft to provide food for hungry villagers or a store for smuggled goods.

The 5 miles (8km) from the headland above Port-Eynon Point to Worms Head is along the broad and airy clifftop. There are a few lower-level paths above the foreshore, but they are generally

not continuous, and the most straightforward route is along the top, passing a succession of fields and occasionally dipping down to round a cove or depression. Half way along you pass above Paviland Cave where, in 1823, a headless skeleton was discovered, along with the remains of a mammoth, woolly rhinoceros and reindeer. The skeleton was pronounced female and because it was stained with red ochre became known as the Red Lady of Paviland. Later tests revealed that she was a he, and radiocarbon suggested the bones dated from 22,000 BC.

The Wriggling Worm

Finally, you reach what's known locally as the Worm, described by Dylan Thomas as 'the rock at the world's end'. The unusual name comes from the Old English for dragon (*wurm*) and, if you use your imagination, the lumpy line of rocks tapering out into the sea could indeed be a serpent wriggling out into the waves. On the furthermost rock, called Outer Head, there's a well-known blow hole which, if the sea is crashing in, periodically produces a strange booming and moaning sound, giving rise to the local saying: 'The old Worm's blowing, time for a boat to be going.' For 2½ hours either side of low tide you can walk across the causeway to see for yourself, but you must make it back in time. Heed the official notice pinned to the former coastguard lookout hut on the mainland cliff opposite Worms Head: 'If you do get cut off, don't try to swim or wade back – you won't make it.'

Above: Worms Head derives its name from the Old English wurm *meaning dragon.*

Below: The small tidal island of Burry Holms sits at the northern tip of Rhossili Bay.

Rhossili itself is a small but popular centre, with cafés and a few shops. The National Trust's visitor centre by the car park has a permanent exhibition about Rhossili and the Gower (open daily; weekends in winter).

It has to be said that the clifftop view from the village northwards across Rhossili Bay is stupendous. A long, straight strip of golden sand disappears into the distance, and at low tide the wooden skeleton of the *Helvetia*, driven ashore in a gale in 1887, sticks out of the sand. The bay is backed by the formidable barrier of Rhossili Down. A broad track goes across its top

LAVERBREAD – AN EDIBLE SEAWEED

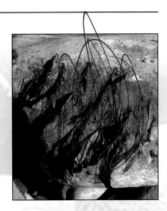

Wandering along the beaches of the Gower on a sunny weekend it's very pleasant to stop at one of the many cafés for refreshment. At some locations, such as Port-Eynon, you may also find a mobile van selling fresh, locally caught seafood, including mussels and shrimps, and cockles from the famous beds at nearby Penclawdd. Also on sale is another, more unusual item, something of a delicacy in this part of Wales. Laverbread takes its name from the Welsh *bara* (bread) and *lawr* (down or foot), and is an edible seaweed, *Porphyra umbilicalis*, which grows best where open sand has fresh water running past it. The seaweed is harvested from rocks in local estuaries and bays between October and May, and in describing the method of its preparation the friendly woman in the van put me in mind of handwashing an exceptionally grubby garment. First you rinse and wash the seaweed four times in fresh water to get rid of the sand, after which it is boiled in a giant cauldron for as much as 15 hours. By then it's reduced to a black, pulpy mass, which is finally minced and ready to eat. Such is its popularity in this area of Wales that there are several processing plants in Swansea that supply major supermarkets, and it is even canned and sold in such prestigious outlets as Selfridges in London. Laverbread is usually fried and served with bacon or sausage, or more traditionally spread on toast with oatmeal or malted vinegar. I am told it tastes better than it looks.

(and another along its foot on the grassy shelf above the beach, if you want to avoid the sand). The open, windy downland includes Sweyne's Howes, two megalithic tombs that were supposedly the burial place of Sweyne, the Scandinavian sea lord who is reputed to have given his name to Swansea. The windy summit of Rhossili Down (633 feet/193 metres), the highest spot on the Gower, is where the old red sandstone juts through the carboniferous limestone, and offers 360-degree views across the whole peninsula. On most weekends, paragliders can be witnessed flinging themselves off the top, while on the beach far below you will meet surfers, swimmers, walkers, sunbathers and fishermen all going about their business. At the far tip of the bay is Burry Holms, a tidal island incorporating the ruins of a medieval monastic settlement, although the building you can see today was rebuilt in the 1850s as a rectory.

Now you swing eastwards on a path across the top of the dunes, with views across the estuary of the River Loughor to Burry Port and Pembrey Forest. Below you the rocky shore includes several caves, a natural arch and the Blue Pool, a lovely tidal rock pool, about 15 feet (4.6 metres) in diameter and used by swimmers when the sea is out. They say that gold doubloons from a 16th-century Spanish galleon have been found in the pool – it's that special! Eventually, the path becomes an easy boardwalk that curves round to a caravan park at Broughton Bay. After following the waymarked public footpath through the site you can continue along the broad sandy sweep of Broughton Bay to Llanmadoc and on along the edge of the saltmarsh to Landimore and Llanrhidian.

The other option, favoured by the author for a reason that will become obvious very shortly, is to wander up the lane from the caravans to Llangennith, about a mile away. Here, overlooking the village green, is the King's Arms pub, open all day in the main holiday season, and serving a cracking pint of beer and a decent plate of food. Cheers!

Index

Picture Acknowledgements

Page 119 (top): Chris Gomersall
Pages 117, 118 & 119 (bottom): Andrew McCloy/Penny Edmonds
Page 157: Malcolm Storey, www.bioamages.org.uk

Author Acknowledgements

Thank you to everyone who helped with the making of this book, including Penny Edmonds, Liz McCloy, Pat and Tony Strelitz, Chris Tyler and Alison McLennan (RSPB), Cathel Morrison (John Muir Trust), and the various local authority officers who supplied expert advice and information.